JIM CONWAY

Friendship

SKILLS FOR
HAVING A FRIEND,
BEING A FRIEND

PYRANEE
BOOKS

Zondervan Publishing House
Grand Rapids, Michigan

FRIENDSHIP
Copyright © 1989 by Jim Conway

Pyranee Books
are published by Zondervan Publishing House
1415 Lake Drive, S.E.
Grand Rapids, MI 49506

Library of Congress Cataloging-in-Publication Data

Conway, Jim.
  Friendship.

  "Pyranee books."
  1. Friendship—Religious aspects—Christianity. 2. Friendship. I. Title.
BV4647.F7C66   1989   158'25   88–33892
ISBN 0-310-51490-8

Printed in the United States of America

89   90   91   92   93   94   95 / DH / 10   9   8   7   6   5   4   3   2   1

They were my Sunday-school teachers, youth-group leaders, confidantes, and prayer warriors.

Their cottage on Rex Lake (Ohio) gave me the opportunity to be fully a boy, enjoying the marvels of God's creation in a turtle, the moon across the water, the wind in willow trees, and the excitement of being the first person to paddle a canoe on the rippleless lake as the sun rose.

Their warm smiles filled the room as our extended family met in their home on Thanksgiving, Christmas, and other holidays to enjoy the warmth of belonging.

Their ready hugs and affirmation of their love and God's love were frequently followed by a question, "How are things with you spiritually?" They were ever present, praying and persuading me to give my life to Jesus. Later they were the strategic part of the human equation that resulted in my call to ministry.

They, being dead, yet live in my heart, my relationships, and my work.

Contents

Part One

GETTING READY
FOR FRIENDSHIPS

Chapter 1

Listen to Me

Hi! My name is Jim and I'd like to have you think of me that way. I'd rather you didn't think of me only in the limited terms that describe me on the cover of this book—those of writer, seminary professor, and pastor.

You see, I'm like many people; I try to put the best stuff out front. Even though those descriptions are true, they don't really tell you much about who I am as a person.

I've learned that people feel closer to me and I feel closer to them when we stop trying to impress each other. So before you start to read this book, please listen to me—to the other parts of me. I hope learning about me will help you be better able to experience deeper friendships.

I'm Afraid

For starters, let me tell you that I'm afraid to write this book. I've looked at many of the other books about friendship, and I've asked God, "Why should I write this book?" In fact, about nine months ago when I first tried to start it, I blocked out a period of time, gathered together notes and books that I wanted to use to enrich the book, and was all set to go. On the day I was to start writing, however, an advertisement came in the mail about a new book on friendship. I was so devastated that I scrapped my entire project.

A couple of weeks later, my wife, Sally, and I had dinner with Ron, a trusted friend who had first helped me start writing books when he was an acquisition editor. Ron sensed I was discouraged and encouraged me to talk about my frustrations. "What you want to say," he said, "is different from what other authors are saying. Don't be intimidated by what's already been written. Go ahead and write it the way you feel." So here we go.

Always the Outsider

You also need to know that I continue to struggle with a poor self-image. It's rather funny that people look at me as successful and "all together." Yet deep within me is a nagging sense of insecurity that comes from my childhood.

I realize lots of people grew up with some of the same problems I had, but that doesn't change the reality that I felt insecure. My insecurity didn't start to go away until I became a Christian a few months before I entered college.

As a child, I felt I didn't belong in the world of people. It was as if I had come from another planet where the creatures didn't understand relationships. Now I was here on earth but without the foggiest idea about how to make friends.

I never did quite figure out how to relate to people. I didn't feel as if I belonged in the world or that people liked or wanted me.

The first school I attended was in Maple Heights, Ohio. I remember frequently standing against the building in a sheltered corner of the playground during recess periods, watching the other kids play together. I was the loner. I was the outsider.

Some People Are Born More Equal Than Others

We moved into Cleveland and Ross became a friend. Ross was a year older than I, bigger, confident and outgoing, and attractive to all the girls. He was a born leader and was very intelligent. In many ways, Ross was everything I wanted to be, and I was honored that he considered me his friend.

Still, even though Ross was my friend, I felt insecure. Yes, he was my friend, but could I depend on that? Would I always be his most important friend?

People with poor self-images expect the worst—and the worst always comes along. Ross was interested in magic and met another friend who shared this interest. I was left out. "Alone again, naturally," as the song says. This experience reinforced my feeling that I didn't belong.

Disappearing Friends

Then there was that big neighborhood snowball fight. It started in Ross's backyard. Ross and I were inside the fence with other boys, and an equal number of boys were on the outside. It had begun as a friendly, though very competitive, fight. Unfortunately, it turned vicious.

The fight went on for hours. As it got dark, I noticed that a number of our guys had deserted, joining the boys on the outside of the fence. Pretty soon I was the only one left. Even Ross had disappeared. The boys on the outside decided to come over the fence and "finish me off."

I was angry at being deserted. My snowballs could not stop the attack. In desperation, I grabbed a small wooden chair and angrily smashed it over the head of one of the boys coming over the fence. You can imagine what happened next. I really took a beating that night, physically and emotionally. I lost the snowball fight. I lost what little status I had. I lost a friend. I remember walking home through the dirty gray snow to a late dinner and crying because I felt so terribly alone.

Sexy Eleven-Year-Old

I was no better off at romance. There was this terrifically cute girl in Miss Listel's fifth-grade class. I mean she was a knockout for an eleven-year-old! Unfortunately, I only loved her from afar because she was in love with Jimmy. He was another one of those intelligent, good-looking, big boys. (You have to remember I was the shortest boy in my class.) All Jimmy had to do was smile at girls and they fell at his feet.

My blond dream and Jimmy went ice skating on the pond across from the school. They probably did it only once or twice, but to me it seemed as if they were always together. So I decided to learn to ice-skate.

Unfortunately, my borrowed skates didn't fit. I must have looked like a clown act as I skated more on the sides of the skates than on the runners. I felt like a jackass.

At Christmas I decided to give this blond jewel of femininity a gift. For several weeks before Christmas (honestly, I feel foolish telling you this) I carefully cut out the paper dolls and dresses that appeared in every Sunday's paper. I made a Christmas card, put all of these accumulated dolls and dresses in it, and gave it to my dream girl. She opened it up, threw the paper dolls and dresses on the floor, and exclaimed, "What do I want with this junk?"

You see, there it was again. It verified for me that I didn't know how to relate to people. No one really wanted to be my friend. I felt I was a strange caricature that God had brought into the world to torment people.

High-Grade Moron

Academically, I was also a failure. I was a low-C student. When I finally graduated from high school, I was third in my class—third from the bottom.

When I had to take a test, I would say to myself, "You know you're going to fail this one just as you've failed all the others. What's the use?" I was sick on the day when I took my IQ test and fell asleep during part of the exam. As a result, I was ranked as a high-grade moron.

With every failure, I realized I didn't belong in the world of successful and beautiful people. The more I believed my failures, the less I tried to make friends and the less I was interested in succeeding.

As I look back at my life up through my teen years, I'm amazed at the repeated intervention of God and the repeated attempts of people to reach out to me, even when I felt so inadequate, inferior, and alone in the world.

Life Is Hard—But There's Hope

This book comes out of my struggles with friendships and is my attempt to say to you, "I want to be your friend." I want you to know there is hope. If you are going through some tough times now or if it's been rough all your life, I want you to know that I understand—I've been there, and I still struggle with my self-image.

I also want you to know me. I want you to know that the things we'll share in this book are not just cute ideas that I thought would look good in a book. I feel your hurt—because I also bleed.

I'm not sitting off in an ivory tower with everything all together. I continue to bear marks from my childhood and from each stage of my life where I've had both successes and failures in relationships.

I also want you to know that week by week I pray for all of the people who read anything I've written. I'm asking God for his blessing on your life.

If you feel like the university student who wrote this bit of verse, then the rest of this book is for you.

Tomorrow, But Not Today

> *I'm not a shoe*
> *tossed in a corner*
> *or an island*
> *lost in the sea,*
> *I'm not an orphan*
> *or an unwanted pet,*
> *but I might as well be,*
> *because I'm alone.*

The student, even though surrounded by people, feels alone. The result is withdrawal into a private world of deeper aloneness. Yet everyone else seems so happy and comfortable. Listen to this pathetic self-disclosure:

> *I pretend to be happy,*
> *and warm and comfortable, too . . .*
>
> *And yet I can't talk about it . . .*
>
> *I feel like a withered left hand*
> *hiding behind someone's back.*[1]

Throughout this book, as we talk together, I'll suggest projects to help your friendship skills grow. Think through the following exercises and take the first easy steps to growing in your friendship skills.

Individual Growth Activities

1. Write out two or three negative experiences from your childhood. As you remember those events, ask yourself, "How have those events influenced my ability (positively or negatively) to make friends?"

2. Now list two or three of the most positive experiences from your childhood and jot down how these experiences affected your friendship abilities.

Group Growth Activities

Note: The group activities should follow the general coaching and outline given for groups in chapter 13 of this book.

Suggestion: Your group will be more effective if you first work through the book personally and then start your group.

1. Use the above ideas as the basis for gradually revealing yourselves to each other.
2. Pray aloud for each other, focusing on the needs and the strengths that were shared.

Chapter 2

This Is Going To Be Fun!

These were the words of Doug, a close friend. For a number of years Doug and I were together on the staff at Twin City Bible Church in Urbana, Illinois. Doug, an extremely creative person, was always enthusiastic about life. It was fun to watch him get charged up over a new idea or a new way of working with people.

On a number of occasions, after we had wrestled with a problem and had come up with some new ideas, he would put his hands together and rub them quickly back and forth. A big grin would spread over his face, his eyes would light up, and he'd exclaim, "Boy, this is going to be fun!"

Doug was not only thinking of the benefit of a problem solved, but of the people who were going to be helped. Doug enjoyed the process of living and was energized by potential growth and change.

As I chat with you through this book, I'm also thinking, "Boy, this is going to be fun!" It will be fun to talk to you, pray for you, and anticipate your growth. All kinds of images are running around in my brain. I see visions of you relating to people in ways you never thought possible. I see puzzled looks on the faces of other people as they ask themselves, "Is this really the same person? What brought about such a change?" I can almost feel the warmth that will come from others because you will have learned some things about how to be a friend. Envisioning your changing life really turns me on. This really is going to be fun!

Get in Touch With Yourself

Briefly, let me tell you what we'll attempt to do. I'll begin by having you invest your feelings in this process. How did you feel when you read the first chapter? Closer to me or farther away? How do you feel about Doug? What are your initial feelings about the rest of this book? Use your mind for more than processing ideas. Use it to process your feelings.

Another thing I hope will happen is that your guilt will be reduced. Relax. In this book I won't say, "You don't have friends because you don't try hard enough—or you're not spiritual enough—or you're a nerd."

My conviction is that people don't have friends because they don't have relational skills or they only use their minds for ideas instead of understanding their feelings.

Forget Guilt

So this is not a book about guilt. You were born as a warm, caring, outgoing human being. Somewhere along the line, that warm, caring person was not encouraged. In other words, you learned not to relate. Whatever you learned can be unlearned. You can learn new skills!

When I was in my late twenties, I went through a Red Cross training program which qualified me as a water-safety instructor.

The course required competence in several different swimming strokes plus knowledge of water rescue techniques and first aid.

What I remember most about my instructor in his midfifties was his big grin and his encouraging philosophy of teaching. Again and again he told us, "If the student doesn't learn, the instructor hasn't taught." He went on to say, "I assume that you're motivated because you're spending your time and money to be here. I'm not going to lay guilt on you about your motivation. I'm going to assume that if you have trouble in this course, then you don't know how to overcome the problem. It's my task to teach you how to swim and how to instruct other people." Wow! What a relief that was for me and the whole class.

He took a lot of the responsibility on himself. He left an impression on me that I want to pass on to you. Relax. I assume you picked up this book because you want to grow in the area of friendship. I assume you are motivated. I assume you want to grow and change. The problem is that you don't know how. That's my job—to teach you.

Exciting or Frightening

I have a sailboat, a sixteen-foot catamaran. I love the water and I love to sail. It's therapeutic for me. I also love to talk about sailing.

Suppose for a moment that you have never been on a sailboat and have never read anything about sailing. But you've been down to a harbor on a number of occasions and watched those graceful sailboats glide along. Frequently you've said to yourself, "Boy! I'd like to do that sometime."

What if I were to say, "My boat's tied up at the marina. Here are the gate keys, the sailbags, and other equipment. Go enjoy yourself on the ocean." If you've never been taught to sail, you might be very frightened. It's okay to dream about sailing, but to actually do it without any training could be sheer terror for you and chaos for everybody else. I gasp as I see you in my mind's eye, bouncing my sailboat off one boat then another, punching holes in their sides as you get yourself out to sea.

For the person without friends, trying to build friendships without knowing how to do it is something like trying to sail without training and experience.

Empty Suggestions

Sometimes people say, "Well, if you want to have friends, you've got to be friendly," or "Why don't you just get out and make friends instead of sitting around here alone all of the time?" The problem with those suggestions is that friendless people don't know how to make friends or they would have done it already. Those are not helpful suggestions!

The very fact that people pick up a book like this or bring up the subject of friendship with another person is because they don't know how to sail the friendship boat and they want to improve their skills. It's really a cry for help.

I want you to know I believe you're sincere, you're reaching out, you're saying, "Please help me." The purpose of this book is to give you the skills you need to be able to have friends.

Remember, having difficulty in relating to people doesn't mean that you are a bad person or that you are unspiritual. The very fact that you are reaching out indicates a great deal of maturity and concern on your part.

False Assumptions

Sometimes we make wrong assumptions, such as, "If I could be perfect, I'd be able to relate." This statement is dead wrong because it focuses on perfection instead of reality.

My wife, Sally, and I have several friends who illustrate this. One couple, who has written extensively on parent-and-child relationships, is having a terrible time with their teenage daughter. Another friend, Dave, has spent most of his career working with teenagers, yet he has never had a real father relationship with any of his three children.

But who am I trying to kid? Sally and I have written a lot about marriage, family, and interpersonal relationships. Yet this morning, just before I started to dictate this chapter, we had conflict. I wanted to be left alone, but Sally had a couple of simple questions to ask. When I came out of my study for a drink of water, she stopped me with her questions, and our different needs collided.

Isn't that crazy? While writing a book about relationships, I blew up at my own wife. Hey, you're not strange. We're in this thing together. Let's learn and grow together.

Skills Not Guilt

You may have some problems. You may need to learn some skills. But you are not a total zero in interpersonal relationships. What we will do is to build on your past successes, no matter how small, and at the same time reduce the potential for failure by teaching you new skills.

So as I said earlier, hang in there. This is going to be fun. Relax! Trust God. Trust yourself. Trust your friends. And trust me as your coach on this pilgrimage.

You see, I'm asking you to open up, to let me into your life to be your coach and friend. I believe you want that. The more you open up, the more possibilities you will see for your own personal growth and the less alienation and loneliness you'll experience.

The great playwright Tennessee Williams once wrote, "If loneliness is as prevalent as we are led to believe that it is, then surely the great sin of our time must be to be lonely alone."[1]

Join your aloneness with the rest of us "lonelies" and let's be lonely together. That idea might even make a great song for Barry Manilow.

I Want to Change Your Thinking

For five years I taught a master's level pastoral counseling course at Talbot School of Theology at Biola University. Each semester I had forty to fifty students who were planning to go into some kind of Christian ministry.

Frequently I said, "Pastoral counseling is not just having a verse of Scripture or an answer for every person's problem; rather, it is learning how to relate to people. Passing this course does not depend so much on reading the books and correctly answering test questions as it does on growing to become a warm, caring human being."

As we share this book experience together, I want you to know—up front—that **I'm trying to change you.** I'm not just interested in giving you new ideas about essential skills. I want to change the way you think about yourself, God, and other people.

I hope you'll drop negative thoughts about your abilities to relate and begin to focus on your strengths and successes. I hope you'll stop thinking of yourself as a 2 in relational skills and that gradually you will say, "No, I'm not perfect, neither is anyone else perfect. I'm growing. Wow, I'm up to a 5 now. I'm learning. I'm practicing."

Trouble Relating to God?

It may sound strange, but sometimes people who have trouble relating to other people also have trouble relating to God. If you see God as a mean, vindictive, out-to-get-you person who enjoys punishing you, you are also likely to view other people the same way.

If you change your view of God, your view of other people will change. The reverse is also true. As you learn to relate better to people, your relationship to God should also improve. I'm expecting your attitudes toward people to change.

The Effect of the Unknown

It may be that you have difficulty relating to people because you're afraid. When we don't know people, it's easy to think negative thoughts about them or even to be frightened of them. It's human nature to "overestimate the evil characteristics of the enemy."[2]

An interesting study was made of American fifth- and sixth-grade children and their attitudes toward Russians. Psychologists showed the children pictures of a Russian road and asked why Russians have trees along their roads. The children suggested, "So that people won't be able to see what's going on beyond the road," and "It's to make work for the prisoners." The children were then asked why American roads have trees along them. The answers were, "For shade," and "To keep the dust down."[3]

New People Are Scary

As you begin to relate to a person, you feel a sense of uncertainty and fear. Do I want to know this person? Does this person want to know me? Will I like her? Will he like me? Do we have anything in common? Remember, it's easier to suspect people when you don't really know them. We put words into their mouths that may not be true at all.

I remember when I first met Chuck Swindoll. We were visiting his church at the invitation of Tom and Betty, who are involved in the leadership there. After the service Tom said, "Come on, let's go up and meet Chuck." I said, "No, I don't think so." I thought, "Chuck Swindoll is this big hot dog who is heard all over the country on radio and has written dozens of books. Why would he want to meet me?"

But Tom wouldn't be put off. He dragged Sally and me up to the front and introduced us to Chuck. I was surprised because Chuck lit up and said, "Wow, I'm glad to meet you. I've read your book *Men in Mid-Life Crisis,* and I've found it really helpful."

Because I'm basically timid, if I had not been urged, I would have missed that opportunity to meet Chuck and the opportunity for a growing number of contacts with him and his wife, Cynthia.

Don't Be a Friend to Everyone

Something else to remember as you change your thinking— you don't need to be a friend to everyone. Remember the model of Jesus. He preached to, ministered to, and healed thousands of people, but he only had twelve disciples. Of those twelve, only three were invited with him when he was transfigured on the mountain.

Don't torture yourself by thinking you have to relate equally to everyone. In fact, don't waste your precious friendship time on relationships that won't be productive.

It's one thing to reach out to a needy person, but it's another to have a friendship. In the first situation you're doing social work or a spiritual ministry of caring. When you are truly a friend, you and your friend will be giving equally to each other. Both of you will be nourished by the relationship.

In your life you should always have some people whom you nourish and who return little or nothing to you. You should also have people who nourish you, but you may return nothing to them. A third kind of relationship is equal sharing. This is friendship.

All three categories are important, but don't refer to the first two as friendships. The first one is your ministry to someone else, the second type is someone's ministry to you. Only the third— equal sharing—is true friendship.

A general rule of thumb in friendships is to look for people who are similar to you. Find people with similar tastes and interests and who have complementary needs. These people are more likely to become your friends. Forget the guilt trip. You don't have to be everyone's friend.

At the same time, remember that it is good for you to know people who are different from you. They expand your understanding of yourself and perception about life. Although they may never become your close friends, they help you to be more rounded.

Give and Receive

Now let's think about the giving and receiving in relationships, which are different sides of the same coin. One reality is that you must be contented with yourself, otherwise you may be continually using your friends to pump you up. After a while the relationship will change so that you will become their ministry rather than their friend.

Think about this idea of liking yourself for a moment. How happy are you with yourself and your life? **Your happiness is your responsibility!** Looking to other people to make you happy is dangerous and moves you away from friendships.

The opposite side of the coin is the danger of being unwilling to receive from friends at times when you have a legitimate need. The flow needs to go both ways. The Bible says, "When the Holy Spirit controls our lives He will produce this kind of fruit in us: love, joy, peace, patience, kindness, goodness, faithfulness, gentleness, and self-control."[4]

Notice that most of these words are relational. That is, someone must give and someone else must receive for the words to have meaning. How can I love you if you don't need love? How can I be patient with you if you don't upset me; or be kind or faithful or gentle with you if those aren't needs in your life?

The Bible also talks about the gifts God gives to us:

> Christ has given each of us special abilities—whatever He wants us to have out of His rich storehouse of gifts. . . . Why is it that He gives us these special abilities to do certain things best? It is that God's people will be equipped to do better work for Him,

building up the church, the body of Christ, to a position of strength and maturity; until finally . . . we will lovingly follow the truth at all times—speaking truly, dealing truly, living truly . . . and each part in its own special way helps the other parts, so that the whole body is healthy and growing and full of love.[5]

But how can others in the body of Christ exhibit the fruits of the Spirit and exercise their gifts if we don't give them the opportunity?

A Gift or Something You Earn?

A seminary student came to me with a problem. His friends had given him a large sum of money to help pay his seminary bills. He didn't know what to do. He felt he couldn't accept the money because he hadn't done anything for them. I encouraged him to allow these friends to exercise their spiritual gifts by giving to him.

Do you ever feel you have to earn a gift? I do. It's hard for me to accept something from someone when I've not earned it.

Now apply these ideas to friendship. If you're going to get yourself ready for friendship, you need to let people love and give to you.

It Doesn't Happen Overnight

Developing friendships is just that—a development, a process. You gradually get to know people and let them know you.

Friendship cannot be accomplished because you read this or any other book. Friendship is not an idea; it's an experience. So if this adventure is going to pay off, you need to make concrete changes in your actions toward other people. Don't worry, I'll coach you.

Be Genuine

You will want to develop genuineness as you relate to your friends. It's important that you are real and sincere.

Psychologist Carl Rogers' counseling methods of listening, being empathetic, and expressing unconditional love have sometimes been criticized. These skills, it is suggested, can all be learned and may not really be part of one's personality.

One critic said,

> Rogerian empathy does not even begin to qualify as sacrifice. First of all, it is a technique that students in clinical psychology learn in graduate school. They are given a list of empathetic phrases to use on clients and are encouraged to memorize them. Then they practice these phrases on one another, using video taping equipment to critique one another's empathy. But Christian love is not a technique to be learned. It is not a skill you hone in graduate school.
>
> Also, the therapeutic context is wrong for sacrifice. The therapist is not sacrificing time and energy; you pay him $65.00 an hour for switching on those empathetic eyes.[6]

I believe that the criticism is too simplistic. The critic's underlying assumptions are that everyone has natural abilities to relate to people and that it is inappropriate to teach people how to relate to others.

It's obvious as we look at the conflicts that exist in churches, in the business world, between neighbors, in family relationships, and between countries, that a great number of people don't know how to establish and maintain relationships. We need to help each other learn to relate.

As you think of developing friendships, however, it's important to ask yourself, "Am I being mechanical in my listening and talking? Or am I a person who genuinely loves and cares for other people?"

Don't Fake It

If you relate to people because you care, because you want to serve and know them, then you won't be a phony. If, on the other hand, you use these skills to manipulate people into being your friends, then you're in deep trouble. You are totally unbiblical.

Don't fake it. Don't exploit people with the new skills you're learning. I'll do my best throughout the book to continually pull you back to genuine relationship skills. But commit yourself now. Say out loud, "I don't want to be a phony. I want to be a genuine friend. I'm not going to use these skills to manipulate people."

At first you may feel that you *are* being phony. That's because it's a new skill and you are not comfortable with it yet.

But this uneasy feeling will pass and your skills will become a comfortable part of you.

Serve, Don't Manipulate

To help yourself become more real, imagine yourself serving other people. Jesus said, "Truly, truly, I say to you, unless a grain of wheat falls into the earth and dies, it remains by itself alone; but if it dies, it bears much fruit."[7]

The manipulative person thinks, "I can use these skills. I can get these people to serve and love me." You must do the opposite. You must love and serve other people. Use your skills to bury yourself in the lives of other people.

After you give some of your life and love to other people, then the other half of the verse will occur; that is, your service to other people will bear fruit. Your friends will become more mature, and they, in return, will enjoy relating to and nourishing you as a friend.

More Than Ideas—Action

As you move through this book, I want you to do more than think about the ideas; I want you to practice them. You'll notice that after each chapter, suggestions are given for discussion questions and practice activities for individuals and groups.

At this point you may be saying, "Wait a minute, what am I getting myself into?" You might even be tempted to stop reading. I can't make you continue reading, nor can I make you do any of the activities. But it's important to remember you can't learn to swim by standing at the poolside watching other people swim. You can't learn to ride a bicycle by watching video tapes or reading books about biking.

I know it's hard. Any new skill is difficult at first. But as you become comfortable with new approaches to relationships, you may look at this experience as the best thing that has happened in your life in the last ten years.

So right now, say to yourself, "I'm willing to give it a go; I'll try it." Remember, I'm only asking you to do the same things that I've gone through in my personal pilgrimage toward friendship.

The Cost Is Time

Recently, while Sally and I were having dinner with our friends Bing and Joann, I mentioned that I was working on a book about friendships. Joann said, "Is there really any hope for helping people develop their friendship skills if you don't get them to change their thinking and actions about time?"

Good point. You see, if you have all of these hot-dog skills and ideas but your life is full of work, activities, and projects, you may never really expand your friendship base.

To put it bluntly, friends take time. Unless your time and lifestyle change, the skills you learn will not be put into action and you'll end up as friendless as before.

The Cost Is Commitment

To me this book is not just a book; it's a part of me. I'm not playing games with you. I ask you not to play games with me.

I'm committing myself to you to do the best job I can to coach you so that you develop the skills and attitudes you need for friendship. At the same time, do more than just read this book. Incorporate these skills and attitudes into the daily flow of your life.

I'm excited about what you're going to do and what you have already done as you've started to think new thoughts.

Sally and I will pray for you as you continue in this growing process of becoming a friend. We're going for a walk now, but let's talk some more when I get back.

Why don't you take a break as well and think about what we've discussed? Use these questions to trigger your thoughts.

Individual Growth Activities

1. How do you feel about **not** being a friend to everyone? (Write out your feelings.)
2. Identify people who only give to you. Identify people to whom you only give.
3. How do your negative or positive relationships now or in the past affect the way you view God and people?
4. When I said, "We are going to practice these skills," what was your reaction? Was it fear? Rejection? Anticipation? Uncertainty? All of the above? None of the above? Briefly write out your reactions.

Group Growth Activities

1. After everyone has had an opportunity to jot down their reactions and feelings to the above questions, break into groups of three and share with each other what you have written.
2. Commit yourselves to pray for each other's personal growth until the next meeting.

Part Two

QUALITIES THAT DRAW FRIENDS TO YOU

Chapter 3

Why We Like People Why They Like Us

Ants are amazing creatures. In Southern California it's a constant battle to keep ants out of our house. I've watched them marching in long lines along the edge of our driveway, along the long sidewalk beside our house, up the side of the wooden fence, across the length of the fence top, down the fence again, across our patio, and into a pinhole opening at the corner of the door frame leading to our kitchen.

I've often wondered who taught them to do that? Did they have march instructors? Did they go to Antville Grade School? It's amazing that ants at birth are ready to work. They are fully developed. They aren't born helpless as we are. Still, they only have a short, limited life while our lives are full of potential. We are able to learn, improve, and develop all through life. **You are not trapped with your present abilities!**

If it is difficult for you to make friends, that doesn't have to limit you for the rest of your life. You do have the potential for growth and change.

In an article entitled "The Psychology of Personal Growth," author Ira Progoff says, "The experiences of Adler, Jung, Rank, and others indicate that neuroses occur in the modern world not because of repressed fears, but because something creative and meaningful is seeking unsuccessfully to express itself in the life of the individual. The frustration of potentiality is the root of neurosis."[1] The implications of this insight are large. We are not a bundle of repressions, but a bundle of possibilities. The key to health lies in reactivating the process of growth.

What Makes Us Human?

As we try to discover what causes us to like other people, we need to think again of those qualities that make us human as opposed to animal. We are human because we interact with people. David Johnson adds depth to our understanding of this by these insights:

> To the extent that our relationships reflect kindness, mercy, consideration, tenderness, love, concern, compassion, cooperation, responsiveness, and caring, we are becoming more human.
>
> In **humanizing** relationships, individuals are sympathetic and responsive to human needs. They invest each other with the character of humanity, and they treat and regard each other as human. It is this positive involvement with other people that we label humane.
>
> In a **dehumanizing** relationship, people are divested of those qualities that are uniquely human and are turned into machines, in the sense that they are treated in impersonal ways that reflect unconcern with human values.
>
> To be inhuman is to be unmoved by the suffering of others, to be unkind, even cruel and brutal. In a deep sense, the way we relate

to others and the nature of the relationships we build and maintain determine what kind of people we become.

There is nothing more important in our lives than our interpersonal relationships. The quality of our relationships, as well as the number, depends on our interpersonal skills. It takes skills to build and maintain fulfilling and productive relationships.[2]

Think for a moment about the people to whom you are attracted. Probably, these people treat you in the positive, human ways just described. As you develop your friendship skills, I'll encourage and teach you how to be more caring, considerate, tender, and responsive—the way God planned for people to relate.

Boo—Are You There?

Sometimes when I'm riding in an elevator, I look around at the people staring at the floor or ceiling. In moments such as that, I want to yell, "Boo!" It's a weird feeling to be with humans, but not have any "human" experiences happening—no one is relating.

Think about your typical day. How many times are you with people yet no relating is going on? What about the people you live with: your family, friends, and neighbors around you? Think about where you work, get gas, buy your food, see a movie, buy your clothes, and worst of all, attend church. Is anything human happening?

Have you been greeted at the door of a church by a smiling usher who gives you a bulletin but doesn't know you? Have you sat next to people in church who don't know you? Have you listened to a preacher, enjoyed the choir, and greeted people after the service but walked away empty? You realize you had been with humans yet none had related to you.

You mechanically shook hands, but no relating took place. Several people said, "How are you?" You responded, "Fine," but no one was really communicating—you each spoke memorized words. You may have experienced a deafening silence of humanlessness in the middle of that crowd. You would have had as much human touch if you watched the service on TV.

Small Steps Move You a Long Way

Part of the process of preparing you to be a friend is that you consciously begin to do human things. In your relationships with people, express

- kindness
- mercy
- consideration
- tenderness
- love
- concern
- compassion
- cooperation
- responsiveness
- caring

Treat people as important. Invest in them the quality of humanity God intended.

Now let's put that in practical form. As you walk down the sidewalk, look into the faces of people, smile, and say, "Hello." As people in stores or restaurants wait on you, glance at their name tags and address them by name. You'll notice that people are pleased when you identify them as more than dispensing machines. Notice their faces light up. Perhaps, as you have more contacts with the same person, a relationship will develop.

Two things take place—one, you enrich that person's life, and two, you begin to build a pattern of being a friend to people. Remember, you may feel awkward at first, but soon you will not even notice you are doing it. But other people will notice.

Why We Like People

An article in *Psychology Today* entitled "The Friendship Bond" revealed the results of a survey of what more than 40,000 readers look for in close relationships. The survey discovered that the most important friendship qualities were loyalty, warmth, affection, and the ability to keep confidences.

A second group of qualities that ranked high on the survey were supportiveness, frankness, and a sense of humor. Items that showed up low on the list were physical attractiveness and similarity in age.[3]

Remember now, these are important insights that we're looking at. Ask yourself, "Am I building the qualities into my life that will make it easy for people to like me?" It's interesting that this survey had physical attractiveness near the bottom of the list.

Other studies show that our physical appearance does influence the way people look at us. One study showed that students judged essays to be worth more if the person was attractive. Juries also conferred less guilt and punishment on attractive people. A study of 17,000 middle-aged men showed that the taller they were, the greater their salary.[4]

In a study by Karen Dion in which college students were shown photographs of people and then asked to guess which ones were the most intelligent, competent, successful, and generally happy—they repeatedly identified the most attractive people as the happiest.[5]

Don't Throw in the Towel

Now don't be discouraged. You may have been born with a large nose like I have or teeth as crooked as mine. On top of that, you might also be as short as I am. (I'm only five-foot-seven.)

You may think you have all kinds of other limitations. But let me point out that these studies show that, although people make their initial judgments of other people on the basis of physical appearance, deep long-term relationships are built on other qualities altogether.

The old saying that "familiarity breeds contempt" is not true. Contempt does not come from familiarity but from discovering, through more frequent exposures to another person, that you really are quite dissimilar. It is dissimilarity that breeds contempt.

Recently Sally and I conducted a national survey of successful married couples for our book *Your Marriage Can Survive Mid-Life Crisis.*[6] We discovered that the couples whose marriages held together over the long run were couples who had a great number of things in common. They shared common attitudes and values, methods of problem solving, and lifestyles.

In fact, people who have ideas, values, and interests dissimilar to ours are generally judged more harshly by us. We "tend to judge them as unintelligent, ignorant, immoral, and even maladjusted."[7]

Why do people like us? The answer is that we are able to keep confidences, we are loyal, we are warm, and we are affectionate. But in addition they also like us because we have similar values, attitudes, and interests. Earlier I encouraged you not to spend your time on fruitless relationships. Look for people who are similar to you and at the same time keep building into your life the qualities of friendship that people are looking for.

Why We Don't Like People

Think for a moment about the people who really turn you off. Be honest. Don't try to cover your true feelings with guilt. Let your emotions give you an accurate reading of people.

Pick out the people that you most dislike. Are you thinking of people who are pushy, controlling, insensitive, and uninterested in you? Have you identified self-centered, insecure, dull, boring, rigid, critical, negative people who seem to hate life, people, God, and everything? Don't forget those who are overly dependent.

The list could go on and on. Here are some of the kinds of people who turn me off:

Egomaniacs. They are always talking about what big deals they are. They're very aloof and arrogant. When I'm in their presence, I feel put down and small. I do all I can to avoid these boors.

Phonies. You never understand who these people are. They're so busy trying to play games with you, that you never get to understand them. Sometimes these people try to figure out what I really want so that they can do or be that for me. I'm suspicious of people like that, because I feel they're trying to earn my love. My love is not for sale; it's a gift.

Sometimes the unreal people are so insecure they try to be like everyone around them. As a result, they are chameleons— one time they're brown, another time they're green. They change values, actions, or lifestyles, depending on who they're with.

By the way, if you've had trouble being phony, practice being yourself, the special person God has made. Then find people who are like you. Don't try to become like other people. You must have an identity of your own. We'll talk more about that in the next chapter.

Pathetics. These people irritate me, yet at the same time I feel sorry for them. Maybe the reason they irritate me is because I feel guilty. I feel as if I ought to help them, but then I get mad at myself for being manipulated by them. Sometimes I'm part of the problem that keeps them dependent because I always jump to their aid.

Pathetic people whine. They complain a lot. Frequently they talk about life with great resignation: "Well, it just never works out for me." Often, you'll hear them sigh, "Oh, I don't know," or they repeatedly take deep breaths.

Many of these people don't even realize they are doing these things. They have learned that if they act pathetic, people will reach out and give them love. They don't believe they're lovable on their own, so they create or expand a problem to get others to love them.

Criticizers. I don't want to be around critical people, especially if they're critical of me. Maybe you have friends like that. You know the kind I mean. They put their hand on your shoulder and say to you, "Now, Jim, I'm saying this to you in Christian love as a brother. I think that God wants you to rethink your views on women in ministry." Did you ever notice that these critical people frequently blame God for the blast they're going to give you?

Research was done on a particular group of people being divided into small groups. Ahead of time some of the people were given information indicating that the group to which they were being assigned wanted them and would like them. Other people were led to believe that their group did not want additional members and might not like them.

Later, the new members were asked about their feelings. The ones who were given positive information before they entered the group, liked being in the group. The ones who were given negative information did not like being in the group.[8] We tend not to like people who find fault with us.

Probably people don't like people for many other reasons. But as you identify a few of the reasons, perhaps you can evaluate your own life and eliminate the detracting attitudes and actions.

The Attractiveness of Jesus

Being a friend means that we enable someone else to reach potentials that they would not have reached without our enabling. This kind of caring is modeled for us by Jesus, of whom the Scripture says, "Who, although He existed in the form of God, did not regard equality with God a thing to be grasped, but emptied Himself, taking the form of a bond-servant."[9]

A Pattern to Follow

The Jesus model of friendship is that of care and understanding which started before we were born and will continue on into eternity. Before we were born, before we knew Jesus as our personal Savior, before we came into a relationship with him, he had already loved us. He started the relationship. He was the first one to love.

Jesus relates to us with qualities of acceptance, empathy, listening, affirmation, and trust. I'm attracted to Jesus because he reaches out to me, affirms and enables me.

The gospels repeatedly picture Jesus as people-centered. He did not so much move from event to event as from person to person. Jesus sacrificed his reputation to minister to people. It didn't make any difference to him whether they were people acceptable to the society or not. His close inner circle of disciples was made up of ordinary fishermen and even a questionable tax collector.

He spent time with a despised Samaritan woman. He was willing to physically touch a leper, even though lepers were supposed to be isolated from the community. Jesus was willing to bear criticism as he took the side of common people against the religious leaders. The religious community thought they were putting him down when they said he was a gluttonous man and a friend of tax collectors, drunkards, and sinners.

Not a "Holy Joe Hot-Shot"

Why have people been so attracted to Jesus down through the centuries? The Bible answers that question in a simple phrase, "We love him, because he first loved us."[10]

As you look at the special relationship Jesus had with so many people, you must be convinced that Jesus is on the side of common people. Anybody who was hurt, sick, mistreated, lonely, disenfranchised, or condemned—people like you and me—were the ones Jesus came to help.

Matthew wrote, "The Pharisees were indignant. 'Why does your teacher associate with men like that?' 'Because people who are well don't need a doctor! It's the sick people who do!' was Jesus' reply."[11] In essence, Jesus was saying, "My job here on earth is to get sinners back to God, not to worry about the good people."

Jesus does not present himself to us as "holier than thou," but rather as a friend. He said, "I no longer call you slaves, for a master doesn't confide in his slaves; now you are my friends, proved by the fact that I have told you everything the Father told Me."[12]

We are not second-class citizens. The Bible says we are part of God's family. Hebrews 4 records that Jesus, who is now in heaven, intercedes for us and that he understands our weaknesses. We are encouraged to "come boldly to the very throne of God and stay there to receive His mercy and to find grace to help us in our times of need."[13]

Your life might be difficult. You might feel that people and the world are against you. But remember that Jesus is on your side. He believes in you. He wants the best for you.

Jesus not only loved people and was on their side, he also served them. Jesus said, "You know that the rulers of the Gentiles lord it over them, and their great men exercise authority over them. It is not so among you . . . just as the Son of Man did not come to be served, but to serve."[14]

Meet Someone's Needs

Jesus serves people now, as he did when on earth. He listens. He's concerned. He wants the best for us. He has our best interest in his heart and wants us to realize our full potential.

Think for a moment about how Jesus serves you. The things you list are also your needs. You need to be loved, to be forgiven, cared for, understood, encouraged, and listened to. Because he meets your needs, you are drawn to him as a friend.

As you understand the needs of people, you are then in a position to reach out and meet those needs. When you meet the needs of people, they will spontaneously be drawn to you. Make sure you underline this next sentence:

Lasting friendships have as their central ingredient the meeting of each person's needs.

Please stop reading this book after you finish these next three sentences. Think of a person with whom you want to develop or deepen a friendship. Now mentally list that person's needs in the following areas:

- social
- physical
- emotional
- spiritual

Think of specific needs in each of the four areas before you continue reading.

Thank you for stopping to think. Remember that learning to be a friend means developing skills and changing attitudes. As we continue through the book, I'll encourage you to do a number of little projects, all aimed at changing your thinking and lifestyle. Stopping to specifically think of a friend's needs is an important part of your process toward growth.

What You Believe Affects Your Behavior

It's commonly accepted in many circles that if you change people's beliefs, their attitudes and actions will automatically change.

That concept is both true and false. Many people say, for example, that they believe they ought to stop drinking or smoking, but they don't. Many people believe in friendships, yet they don't have friends. Why is this?

The reason is that ideas and beliefs must be tied to our current needs and life experience or they will not become part of our personality, actions, and attitudes.

If you, right now, have a deep need in your life to develop better friendships, then that need will cause you to keep reading, thinking, and practicing so that your attitudes and actions will be changed.

Your Teachable Moment

Other people have no need or desire to improve their friendships. As a result, they won't pick up this book; if they did, they would lightly skim it, because the topic is not immediately appropriate to their needs.

When you have a need in your life, a vacuum is created. Almost involuntarily you begin searching for people, ideas, attitudes, different lifestyles, or other ingredients to fill that vacuum.

During the time that you have a vacuum or a need in your life, you are open to grow. You are at a "teachable moment" in your life. You are ready to give change a whirl even though it may be uncomfortable, new, or frightening.

How It Works

For example, later in the book I will teach you how to listen. If you really have a need to grow in the area of friendships, then you will drink in and absorb what I'm going to talk about. You'll even be willing to practice the listening skill.

In fact, what will happen as you practice listening is that you will have a new belief structure about the importance of listening. Listening will become so much a part of your life that you'll find yourself spontaneously practicing it.

Behaviors do influence your beliefs. The more you practice

listening and see the benefits of it, the more you will believe in the importance of listening.

So I will keep on pushing you to think new thoughts about friendships and also to put into practice friendship skills that will meet the friendship needs of your life. Before you move to the next chapter, practice a bit of what you have been reading by using the following activities.

Individual Growth Activities

1. List the two or three traits in other people that most turn you off.
2. List the two or three traits in other people that most attract you.
3. Look over your two previous lists and circle the negative or positive traits that are part of your own personality. Identifying these traits now will give you perspective as you begin to develop your friendship skills.
4. From your personal experience in knowing God, which of his traits most attracted you to him?
5. In daily prayer thank God for the positive qualities in your life and ask him to change the negative.

Group Growth Activities

1. Discuss with the group your lists from activities 1 and 2 from the Individual Growth Activities. Then share how each of these negative or positive traits makes you feel. Who are you reminded of from your past as you see this trait in a person today?
2. Share with the group which trait you would most like to keep and which one you want to change.
3. In groups of two or three pray aloud for each other.

Chapter 4

What Do I Think of Myself?

Most people who have trouble with friendships also have poor self-images. So if you are going to grow in your ability to make friends and keep them, then we've got to tackle your self-image. Talking about self-image is painful for me because it reminds me of the struggle with low self-esteem that I have had and to some degree continue to have.

My parents have told me that they wanted me—but I did not feel wanted. I did not feel successful in school or in relationships with other people. I didn't like myself nor did I like the way I didn't seem to fit into the world of people.

As a result, I experienced what's called a "self-fulfilling prophecy." What I thought of myself actually limited me so that I repeatedly failed. This, in turn, reinforced the fact that I wasn't worth anything and, therefore, would fail again.

In junior high school I was required to memorize Shakespeare's Sonnet 29. Shakespeare captured exactly what I felt of

myself. Unfortunately, many people who have trouble with
friendships think the same of themselves. Read through the first
part of the sonnet to see if you find yourself there:

> When, in disgrace with fortune and men's eyes,
> I all alone beweep my outcast state,
> And trouble deaf heaven with my bootless cries,
> And look upon myself, and curse my fate,
> Wishing me like to one more rich in hope,
> Featured like him, like him with friends possessed,
> Desiring this man's art and that man's scope,
> With what I most enjoy contented least.

If you are struggling with a poor self-image, you probably
also think that you're the only one who struggles with it. That's
why I wanted you to know something about me. You're not in the
boat alone. The world is filled with people who never realize their
potential, who are afraid to take risks, who struggle with
relationships, and who don't like themselves.

In the book *Irregular People,* Joyce Landorf talks about people
who have had tragic limitations in their lives which have limited
their ability to relate with or love people.[1] When you come down
to it, each human being is an irregular person because we've all
experienced limitations, struggles, trials, and disappointments. All
of these negative events or people have influenced the way we
relate or fail to relate.

I'm Bad and God Is Mean

People with poor self-images tend primarily to see the
negative in life. When you make a list of your positive and
negative traits, which list is longer? Probably your negative list.

People with poor self-images go through the day seeing more
bad than good. To them, half of the pie is gone rather than half of
the pie is there to be enjoyed.

Christians who have poor self-images tend to interpret the

Bible pessimistically. They tend to see God in a negative light.
Maybe you've found yourself singing the song,

> You'd better watch out,
> You'd better not cry,
> You'd better not pout,
> I'm telling you why,
> The big mean God is comin' to town.

How We Got the Way We Are

Genesis 1 records that God created everything with the
capacity to reproduce its own kind. In practical terms, that means
that you and I and every living critter in the world take after our
parents.

Family. I have a fairly good-sized nose, but that's to be
expected. In fact, you should have seen Frank, my grandfather.
He looked like Jimmy Durante with the same large nose and ears.
I have often joked that my wife prays daily for God not to let that
part of my genetic history come through, resulting in my nose and
ears getting bigger with age.

You've got a combination of the physical characteristics of
your parents. Maybe you like parts of your body and hate other
parts. We are the products of our ancestors, for good or bad. We
inherited our parents' appearances along with some of their
emotional, intellectual, and spiritual characteristics. These qualities, which may be benefits or handicaps, are not of our choosing.
Nevertheless, they are part of us.

Environment. Our lives have also been profoundly affected by
our life experiences thus far. One of the positive memories I have
from my childhood was my warm, caring grandparents, Frank
and Mary, who took a personal interest in me. They were a
significant part in my positive development. They taught me how
to tackle hard jobs, introduced me to Jesus, and taught me to hear
God's call into ministry.

I also had frightening experiences. One morning, on my way to grade school, I fell out of my father's car when we were going more than fifty miles an hour. I was so concerned that he might leave me that, in spite of my injuries, I jumped up and started running after the car.

I also remember going along the railroad tracks with my mother, picking up pieces of coal that friendly trainmen threw off so that we could keep warm in the winter. I remember the Depression, summers at Rex Lake, victory gardens during World War II, camps, Sunday school, and neighborhood kids. All these events have marked me.

You have been marked, not only by your genetic background but also by the environment in which you were raised. The people who affirmed you gave you a positive view of other human beings. The people who put you down or belittled you have caused you to feel uncertain about yourself and others.

Probably your struggle with friendships has a profoundly strong link to the negative events and people in your own developmental process.

Now I want to caution you: Don't give up. You might be thinking, "Well, I did have some bad things in my background. My parents really didn't know how to relate. Maybe I'm stuck. Maybe I'll never be any different."

Genesis 1 tells us that God created living things to bring forth after their own kind. Not only are we likely to look like our parents, but it is also inferred that we will respond to life as our parents did. But take heart. The Bible also says, "God created man in his own image."[2] You were not only created in your parents' image, but also in God's.

Yes, you have your past, but you also have God. Remember the classic verse: "Therefore if any man be in Christ, he is a new creature: old things are passed away; behold, all things are become new."[3]

You Can Change

You are not trapped with your old experiences and genes. You do have the capacity for change! You can be different! But I won't kid you. You must take charge of your life! You must stop saying, "I'll never be different," and begin saying, "I can be different because of God's love working in me."

If you've invited Christ into your life, you have been reborn and the Holy Spirit is working to help you become all that God wants you to be.

Limitations of a Poor Self-Image

Most of your choices, your successes, or failures, can be directly tied to what you think of yourself. I mentioned that I was a poor student in school. Before starting an exam, I would tell myself I was going to fail because I had failed every exam in the past. As a result, I continued to fail.

Have you had experiences like that at school or work? Do you remember when you were a teenager and looked at that really good-looking guy or girl? You wanted him or her to notice you. You wanted to be friends, perhaps even date—but your self-image said, "Don't even think about it. That person is so much better than you. You're not even worthy to clean that person's toilet let alone go on a date."

Could It Be True?

In a junior high study hall I remember Janet, a pretty girl with flashing brown eyes, a big smile, an outgoing personality, and a great body. But she didn't know I existed. In the study hall, I'd look over the top of my book and just drink in her beauty.

One day she looked up and smiled. I turned around to see who she was smiling at. I was sitting against the wall; no one else was there. Janet was smiling at me. I smiled back. Was I dreaming? Was this true?

The following day I tried it again. Janet was looking at me, unbelievable as it might be. Remember, I basically thought of myself as short and ugly, not a macho hunk that any woman would desire, especially not this smashing beauty.

The deliriously wonderful outcome was that I dated Janet several times. She had a strong impact on improving my self-image. She also was responsible for encouraging me to go out for the track team, which also helped me to feel better about myself.

Your poor self-image may hold you back and limit your life in the same way mine has been limited. Friendships will become one of the keys for changing your self-image.

Negative Self-Talk

One of my high priorities for you is to improve your view of yourself. You may not realize it, but your self-image is already starting to improve as we spend time talking in this book. However, your inner self carries on a conversation of its own and it may sound like this:

"I think other people are like me." Your low view of yourself screens and limits your understanding of others. You attribute qualities to people that are the same qualities you possess. If you're a suspicious person, you'll tend to see suspicion in others. If you're insecure, you may project onto others an exaggerated sense of insecurity or as having it all together. In either case, your poor self-image creates a false illusion that people are either better or worse than they really are.

"I think the compliments of other people are false." A bad self-image imposes a barrier that causes you to distort what you think other people think of you. Your distortion is usually more negative than true. You might say to yourself, "They couldn't really like me. They think I'm dumb. They're laughing at me."

Your poor self-image may even twist the truth that comes from other people. If someone gives you a compliment or affirms you with a smile, you might brush it off, perhaps even question their honesty. "They must not be telling the truth. They're just playing games with me. They don't really like me." The tragedy is that all of the affirmation that could bolster your self-image is actually being rejected and only reinforcing your poor self-image.

"I think I can only be or do this." A poor self-image is like a baby's playpen. All of the baby's activities are limited to that playpen. The baby can look at the outside world, watch brothers or sisters play, but still not get out of the playpen.

The Self-Defeating Cycle

A poor self-image is self-defeating. It gives you a distorted view of yourself and of the world around you. It manipulates your life and relationships. Frequently, sad to say, other traits are attached to a poor self-image.

Insecurity. If you feel that you are not quite worthwhile, then you think that other people are better than they are. This view reinforces your feelings of inadequacy and insecurity.

Perfectionism. It may sound strange, but frequently a person with a poor self-image tends to be a perfectionist. If you feel inadequate, unsure of other people's love, then you start saying to yourself, "If only I try harder, if I achieve more, if I'm a better person, then I'll feel better about myself and other people will love me."

Perfectionism, however, is never satisfied! If you can't accept any good things that people say of you, then even if you do great things, your accomplishments will not satisfy that insatiable, gulping appetite of perfectionism.

The perfectionist never asks the question, "How much is enough? At what point can I stop? How much perfection will I have to accomplish to receive the love from people that I really want?" There never is an end; only God is perfect.

The perfectionist also fails to realize that God loves unconditionally. God doesn't withhold love until we arrive at perfection. He loves us while we are growing and even while we are his enemies. His love enables us to change and mature.

Tragically, perfectionists think other people will like them better for their perfection. But truthfully, it is just the opposite. People like to be around flexible, tolerant, imperfect people—like themselves. Perfect people frighten them and cause them to withdraw.

Perfectionists are always paying a debt. The irony is that no one is asking that any debt be paid. Perfectionists do all of this because their poor self-images manipulate them into doing it.

Pride and humility. People with poor self-images struggle with the whole pride-humility conflict. They have a desperate craving to be valued—to be worth something to somebody. There is a grasping for affirmation. As a result, sometimes people with poor self-images appear to be boastful, even arrogant.

Insecure people, however, struggle at the same time with humility. Their personalities cry out for affirmation, but their poor self-images tell them that they aren't worth anything anyway. Their feelings say they aren't being humble if they want affirmation. They experience a constant yo-yoing of desires and present a confused picture of their pride and humility.

Truly healthy people are able to express both pride and humility by recognizing that they do have special gifts and abilities. But they also recognize that these gifts and abilities are not of their own creation but are an endowment from God.

A good blend of both pride and humility is shown in the mature expression of the apostle Paul when he says, "But by the grace of God I am what I am, and his grace to me was not without effect. No, I worked harder than all of them—yet not I, but the grace of God that was with me."[4]

Paul was not saying, "I am a worthless worm." He was not denying his impact in the world as he ministered to people, but at the same time he expressed humility by recognizing that the gifts and opportunities he had been given, came from God.

In the next chapter I want to think with you about positive traits in the mature person. I will coach you in the maturing process so that immaturity, poor self-image, perfectionism, false pride, and false humility don't get in the way of your friendships. But first think through the following activities.

Individual Growth Activities

1. If you have struggled with a poor self-image, list two or three of the causes or sources as you see them.
2. List ways in which your poor self-image causes you to devalue other people or yourself.
3. List a few ways that your poor self-image has caused you to inflate yourself or other people.
4. Write yourself a letter from God. Tell yourself how much God loves you and what God is going to continue to do in your life. Read the letter each day for a week, adding to it and thanking God for his love.

Group Growth Activities

Share information from the above list with the group. After each person shares, encourage the group members to affirm the person by sharing a positive statement of encouragement. (Make sure that no one is left unaffirmed.)

Chapter 5

The Maturing Person

Some years ago Martha, a married woman in her thirties, shared with me her frightening secret. After several embarrassing attempts to talk, she finally revealed that she was abnormally sexually attracted to men. After Martha had spilled out her problem, she kept her head down. I think she was waiting for me to condemn her. I told her it was okay to talk to me about this problem. I was still her friend, and I would not share it with anyone unless she gave me permission.

Martha assured me that her sexual life with her husband was fine. Intellectually and spiritually, she knew she should not feel this way. "I have no desire to get involved with another man. After all, I have a happy home and marriage, three wonderful kids, and I'm the chairperson of the deaconesses in my church."

After a long silence she shared more about her dreaded compulsion. "I feel vulnerable to the attentions of other men. In fact, if an attractive salesman came to my door when the kids weren't home and he made flirtatious advances toward me, I'm afraid I would go to bed with him."

Martha was horrified at her own words as they echoed in the room. She sobbed uncontrollably. "What can I do? What can I do? These feelings are getting stronger, even though I want them to go away."

For the next thirty minutes she continued to unburden her heart, pleading for help.

Martha needed to mature by understanding who God had created her to be. In this chapter we'll look at the important qualities necessary for maturity and how to cause those traits to be a normal part of your life and friendships. I'll also share what I did to help Martha as well as what helped me to be more mature in my friendships. Let's start by looking at the qualities of a maturing friend.

Qualities of a Maturing Friend

Self-understanding, self-acceptance, self-appreciation. Maturing people are not afraid to understand themselves. The Bible encourages us to be honest in our estimate of ourselves.[1] We are not to overestimate ourselves. As I've said, people with a poor self-image tend to exaggerate themselves. In their fantasy life they imagine they are supermen or superwomen. Overestimating sets people up for perfectionism.

But people with a poor self-image also underestimate themselves. They say, "I can't. I'm not good enough." They fail to count on the power of God and his past successes in their lives.

Self-acceptance enables me to say, "I am what I am."[2] "Yes," I acknowledge, "I do have limitations. But I also have strengths. I refuse to live in a dream world, wishing my life away or envying other people. I refuse to 'curse my fate,' as I quoted from Shakespeare in the previous chapter. Neither do I intend to do as those lines say:

Wishing me like to one more rich in hope,
Featured like him, like him with friends possessed,
Desiring this man's art and that man's scope,
With what I most enjoy contented least."

Self-appreciation enables us to enjoy, value, and prize the uniqueness of our creation. The apostle Paul's statement of himself was, "I am what I am." That's acceptance.

He also said, ". . . by the grace of God."[3] I can appreciate who I am as I see God involved in my unique creation and development. As I recognize God as the continued Creator in my life, I don't struggle as much with the whole humility-pride syndrome. Remember, you can't start any process of self-improvement until you accept who you are now.

Love. Maturing people allow others to love them. They are willing to accept love without having to earn it or pay for it. They allow love from other people to penetrate their personalities and provide the nourishment God intended.

Maturing people, when loved by another person, do not respond with guilt by saying, "Well, now I must be sure to pay that person back with equal love." No! Instead they respond to the loving person by saying, "Thank you, that feels good. I'm glad to be loved by you."

Saying "thank you" allows the other person's expression of love to be absorbed into your personality. At the same time, it provides a positive affirmation to the person who has loved you. If you fail to thank the other one, it indicates you probably aren't allowing that person's love to flow into you. It also indicates a subtle rejection on your part. If your pattern is repeated often, your friend will seek other friends.

Giving love is the other side of the coin. Maturing people do not love out of guilt or manipulation, but because they sense the need in another person's life. Giving love is an opportunity to help another person grow, develop, and become, as John Powell says, "fully human, fully alive."[4] Loving allows your friend to become all that God intended him or her to be.

Giving love, then, is not what makes us feel good or what we would like to have done for us, but it clearly focuses our thoughts and energies on the needs of the other person.

Giving love is modeled for us by God, of whom it was said, "[He] loved the world so much that He gave His only Son so that anyone who believes in Him shall not perish but have eternal life. God did not send His Son into the world to condemn it, but to save it."[5] God isn't doing something for himself; he is providing sacrificially for our best good and growth.

Self-mastery, internal values. Maturing people are not puppets manipulated by the strings of many forces and people, but they are in control of their own destinies. Obviously, this doesn't mean that others don't influence their lives. They choose to allow other people or circumstances to influence them. They are in control of which influences they allow. They are not victims of circumstances; they choose to function on the basis of their own values.

Serving. Maturing people serve other people, not out of guilt nor a hope that they will return love and service. Maturing people view serving as **the** mission of life. They spend their lives enriching the lives of other people. Mature people are not trapped into service with a sense of duty or obligation; service flows naturally because they want to enrich other lives.

Relating. Maturing people have the ability to relate to others. They do not think of themselves as hermits or as islands in the midst of a vast ocean. They think of themselves as spice in an elegant food. They recognize their unique contribution to the lives of other people. They also recognize the importance of other people's contribution, or spice, to their lives.

Intimacy with God. Maturing people recognize that they have been created by God and that the fullness of God's creation will not be realized until they come to have a friendship with God.

You may find it difficult to think of yourself as God's friend. Some of that inability may spring from the same difficulty you have with human friendships. Friendship with God and with humans is similar. If you have a struggle in one area, it probably indicates that you have difficulty in the other.

Now for a moment look back over the six areas of maturity that I've listed. Don't be intimidated; rather, ask yourself, "How am I doing in some of these areas?" Don't let perfectionism take over. Nobody is fully mature. Nobody perfectly matches all of these standards except, of course, God.

Rate yourself in each of these important areas, from 0 to 100 percent:

- self-understanding ____%
- giving and receiving love ____%
- self-mastery ____%
- serving ____%
- relating ____%
- intimacy with God ____%

Remember that anything above zero is positive. For example, if you are 20 percent along in your ability to serve people, don't look at the other 80 percent. Instead say, "Wow! I'm already 20 percent along in my maturing process of serving other people."

In other areas you may find yourself at 5 percent or 40 percent. Remember to say, "Wow! I'm 5 percent on my way." Nobody is 100 percent in any or all of the areas. We are all growing.

Improving Your Self-Image

Let's think together about the process of improving your self-image and moving you toward greater maturity. The following steps will become practical building blocks for this process.

Become a Reflective Person

Becoming more mature and building a strong self-image means that you will need to "devote time to unstructured solitude ... be willing to daydream and speculate, be reflective, consider strengths and weaknesses, along with problems, [and] opportunities ... be willing to express feelings. Allow the mind to freely associate with such phrases as 'I'd like to,' 'I choose to,' 'I have to,' 'I'm afraid to,' or 'I can't.' "[6]

As you become a reflective person, you will more accurately understand who you are. Then you will be able to modify those areas which can be changed or learn to work within your limitations, realizing that you are known and loved by God.

Let me suggest a little project that I've used with hundreds of people as they have worked toward maturity and a stronger self-esteem. Start by making lists in the following areas. Each of your personal lists contains important clues about you and will give direction to your life and friendships.

1. All the things I like to do. List things that are pleasant and fun for you. Remember, no one else has to see this list, so be as honest as possible. Try to include fifty to one hundred items. Develop this list over several days. Maybe your list will include items such as walking, listening to music, biking, reading, or running barefoot in the park. Don't be afraid to include crazy stuff that may be known only to you.

2. All the things I am able to do. List all of the areas in which you have skills and abilities, even if some of these skills are just developing. You might list things you know a lot about that you could share with other people, such as how to transplant a tree, ski, swim, or cook. List everything, even if it seems small or unimportant. Remember, you don't have to show your list to anyone else.

3. The most negative influences, events, or people in my life. List the downers for you. Remember, it's impossible to forgive any person, event, or even God unless you first acknowledge that this was or is a problem for you. Don't cover up. Again remember this is your private list.

4. The most positive influences, events, or people in my life. List the people or events who have made favorable contributions to your life. Then jot a word or two about how these contributed to you.

5. I am most angry at ... This list might include world events, people, situations, or lifestyles. List the items that really anger you.

6. I am most happy with ... Now list things that produce happiness and joy in you.

7. Before I die I want to ... List all the things you hope to accomplish before you die.

Now we both realize that you're not going to whip off these lists all at once. In fact, that's not the best way to do it. Take several days to work on this project. You'll notice as we go along that you will have overlapping projects. Keep working on each one, because improving your ability to be a friend will come from several small changes in your attitudes and skills.

Now, when you get done with your lists, look back over them as if you were an outside observer. Ask, "What kind of person is this?"

You'll notice patterns developing. You'll see the dominant factors, both negative and positive, that formed your life. You'll also begin to spot forces and people that energize your life in positive or negative ways.

As you go through the items on the lists, notice that some items are very similar to each other and indicate a strong tendency in your personality. Make sure that you actually incorporate these desires, abilities, and dreams into your overall lifestyle and relationships. You must live out the dreams and patterns on your

lists or you will experience an uncomfortableness with yourself
that may even verge on hostility, anger, or depression.

Martha Revisited

At the beginning of the chapter I mentioned a woman who
struggled with terrifying sexual temptation. She needed to
respond to all of God's creation in her so that her relationship
with people would not be distorted. At the end of our first session
I suggested she make several of the lists I just encouraged you to
make. I explained in detail what she should do and the kinds of
items that should be included on her lists. They were her private
lists. She would not have to share them with her husband or with
me unless she chose to do so.

We agreed to pray for God's protection during this problem
and for his guidance as she made out her lists. Our plan was to
meet together in two weeks, giving her ample time to keep
adding items to her lists.

When she came back, she was still terrorized by her
temptations. I asked if she would be willing to share any of the
lists with me. She said, "I have written some very private things,
but I trust you as you look at them."

I quickly looked at her lists and noticed certain patterns. I
could detect that Martha enjoyed the out-of-doors, hiking, biking,
camping—she was a tomboy. Yet she was sitting in my office in a
frilly dress.

I asked her what her daily routine included. She assured me
she tried to be a good wife and mother by cooking special foods,
sewing her kids' clothes, and making her own curtains. I
commented, "I don't see any of those things on your lists. Do you
like to do those things? What I do see on your lists is that you're a
tomboy. You like outdoor activities. But you're telling me that
your daily life is all indoor stuff."

Then I drew two circles. "Circle A," I told her, "contains all
of the things that are native to your personality such as the

interests, gifts, and abilities God has given to you. Circle B contains all of the things that you actually do—those 'good-mother-and-wife things.' Ideally, your two circles should overlap. That is, you should be living out the uniqueness that God has given you. I really suspect that this strange sexual temptation is your personality crying out, 'Please pay attention to me. I'm going to force you to think about who you really are.' "

We talked about how she could begin to do items that were in Circle A (who she actually was) so that they became a part of Circle B (what she did). She was willing to share her lists with her husband, Dennis, and we planned to meet with him the next week.

At that third meeting it was obvious that the two of them had shared her fears and her lists. They were working creatively to bring her two circles more closely in line with each other.

They had agreed to buy bikes and to have some evening meals in the park. They were also planning hiking and camping weekends and vacations. It looked as if they were on their way to wholeness. We agreed they would telephone me in about two weeks and let me know what was happening.

About two-and-a-half weeks later Martha called and said, "You'll never believe what's happened. Those strange temptations have almost totally disappeared. My depression is no longer a problem. Life seems to have taken on a totally new meaning. I almost feel guilty because we're enjoying life so much."

I've watched hundreds of people change in similar ways as they have come to understand themselves and bring their lives into line with God's special creation in their lives.

If you were tempted to only read about those lists and not start making them, I would suggest you go back to that section of this chapter about becoming a reflective person. Get your paper and get started. Add items to your lists, day by day, as you think about them. As your lists start to grow, reflect on that information and allow it to bring modifications to your lifestyle.

Accept Affirmation From Other People

A second step in improving your self-image is to learn how to accept affirmation. Whenever someone congratulates you for a good job or tells you that you look nice, you're a thoughtful person, a good friend, or a sensitive individual—whatever their expression of appreciation—accept it. Don't respond by saying, "Oh, it was nothing," "Oh, I'm not really like that," "You don't really know me," or "Wow, that was just a fluke."

Instead, respond by saying, "Thank you very much, I appreciate that," "I'm grateful to have a person like you say something like that to me," or "That's really an encouragement to me." Practice accepting appreciation from other people.

When you absorb other people's affirmations into your personality, you then begin to experience the last half of Shakespeare's Sonnet 29, in which he says:

> Yet in these thoughts myself almost despising,
> Haply I think on thee, and then my state,
> Like to the lark at break of day arising
> From sullen earth, sings hymns at heaven's gate;
> For thy sweet love remembered such wealth brings
> That then I scorn to change my state with kings.

Accept Jesus' Affirmation

Here's another assignment. Over the next several weeks I want you to read through the first four books of the New Testament: Matthew, Mark, Luke, and John.

Thoughtfully reflect on every contact that Jesus had with people. What happened to the people? How did Jesus relate to them? What type of person was Jesus critical of? How frequently did Jesus break tradition to care for people?

Notice his patience and gentleness, his probing and encouragement. Study the accounts of his encounters with people and their reactions. People thought of themselves differently after contact with Jesus.

One of those delightful stories is the account in Luke 19 of that "rather odious little man, Zaccheus."[7] Zaccheus is reported to have been short, and maybe his shortness caused him to compensate by seeking power.

One writer suggests that Zaccheus turned traitor to his own people and acted as an agent for the Romans to amass considerable wealth. Whatever the reason, you will notice that this short man was despised by his countrymen because he was a crooked tax collector.

Zaccheus was fascinated with Jesus. Perhaps he was awed by his power with the people, or maybe he saw in Jesus an opportunity for personal wholeness.

As Jesus moved through the town, he saw Zaccheus up in a tree. But Jesus saw more than that. He saw "a human being, unloved, unloving, bruised, and hurt by the circumstances of life, unsuited to his wealth, . . . unacceptable to those around him, unacceptable to himself."[8]

Jesus then did the unexpected, the dramatic. He invited himself to Zaccheus' house for a meal. Jesus' acceptance of this shriveled little man so overwhelmed Zaccheus that he repented on the spot and promised a changed lifestyle. "Half of my possessions I will give to the poor, and if I have defrauded anyone of anything, I will give back four times as much."[9]

Jesus responded with a statement of affirmation and forgiveness that reinstated Zaccheus not only with God, but with his community: "Today salvation has come to this house."[10] What a great transformation! This man, so rejected by others and himself, found a new acceptance of himself and with God and others.

As you read accounts of Jesus working with a great variety of people, courageously talk to Jesus as you would with any human being. Tell him your needs and ask him to bring about in you the same feelings of love and acceptance that you see taking place in the people of the New Testament.

As you begin to value yourself, to see God's unique creation in you, and to see your unique contribution to the world, you should be able to say to yourself the following five statements.

- **I belong;** I am wanted; I do have a place in the world and with people
- **I have a sense of worth;** I do count for something; I can respect myself
- **I am competent;** I can do certain things, maybe not everything, but I am competent to do some things
- **I have moral and ethical standards;** I know what is right; I do have internal values; I am not a victim or a puppet
- **I do make a difference;** I can influence and change situations and people[11]

Look for opportunities, relationships, books, and experiences that will help you grow in any of these five areas listed above. Now briefly, let me mention some of the things that helped me to grow.

What Helped Me

You already know something about me. The first eighteen years of my life were very shaky as far as my self-image. But then events and people began to make a dramatic impact on me. Perhaps these suggestions can help you to grow so that you will become a more confident person as you relate to other people.

My Relationship With God

Just before I went to college, I gave my life unreservedly to Christ. He started a transformation in me that was very similar to the people's experiences you are reading about in the first four books of the New Testament.

The result was that I didn't think of myself as a pygmy

anymore; rather, I increasingly saw myself as a person with potential. I didn't see myself as a misfit, but as a person who uniquely fits into God's purpose and plan for the world.

God's constant affirmation of me as I prayed, read, and meditated on the Scriptures dramatically affected my life—so much so that my parents couldn't believe that I was "the same Jimmy that went off to college."

Within nine months of giving my life to Christ, I accepted God's call into full-time Christian ministry. Within two-and-a-half years, I was pastoring my first church as a college student. My insecurities and fears were not instantly removed, not at all! But God did start a transformation that continues today. The fears and insecurities that remain today are God's way of keeping me in touch with the world of people who are insecure.

From my point of view, a personal, serious, reflective commitment and daily walk with God can produce rapid maturing and a dramatic change in self-perception.

If you have never started that relationship with God, let me encourage you to do that right now. Say to God, "I'm sorry for keeping you out of my life. I want you to forgive all of my past and even my future failures. I accept Christ's sacrifice as the payment for my wrongs. I want to belong to you. I want you to live in me, to become the center of my life, to provide the direction and dynamism I need. Here's my life, my mind, my will. Make me into the person you want me to be."

Then read the Bible daily. Start with the sections I've suggested, the first four books of the New Testament—Matthew, Mark, Luke, and John. Read about ten to twelve verses a day in a slow, reflective way, asking God to impress ideas on your mind. Watch for any phrases or words that stick out as you read. Stop for a moment and reflect on these key ideas. Talk to God about what they mean for your life that day. This reflective relationship will make you, as the Bible says, "a brand new person inside."[12]

Other People Affirming Me

During my first year in college, I got into a small group of college men. We committed ourselves to pray together for each other every day. Without realizing it, strong bonds of caring, affirmation, and friendship developed. We were each other's best supporters. We drew the very best out of each other. In a sense, we became better than we really were, because we believed in each other.

At the beginning of my second year in college I met Sally. She also believed in me. She loved me and continued the process of affirmation and drawing me out to be God's best. It's important to be around people who believe in you, who will pull, drag, and shove you, if necessary, until you become the most effective person that you can be.

Seeing Other People in Reality

I began to understand that I was not the only person who was in the growing process. No one else in the world was perfect. Everyone else was in the process of developing as I was. I was not a klutz. I was a normal person with normal limitations.

It also helped as I read about great men. Many of them had difficult starts and struggles throughout life. Luther, for example, frequently battled depression. The apostle Paul had some kind of giant limitation that he asked God to remove, but God's response was, "My grace is sufficient."[13]

In fact, I began to see that the normal Christian life was not one without difficulties and limitations but just the opposite. New Testament writers James and Paul both wrote that God has no intention of removing all of the stress from our lives, but he wants us to draw on his strength in the presence of our limitations.[14]

I also learned that God plans to use limitations in my life to make me a more sensitive, gentle, and caring person who is responsive to him and to the needs of other people. I continued to experience great freedom as I realized that everyone is limited and that God uses our limitations as bridges to help others.

My Own Values

As I stopped trying to be like other people and started living according to my own values that God was forming in me, I experienced great freedom and confidence. I didn't have to be like someone else. I could be the unique person whom God was forming me to be. I could stop trying to do everything and feeling inadequate. Now I could start doing the things God had equipped me to do, even though sometimes they were terrifying to me.

Taking Measured Risks

I have found that it is good to push myself just beyond my current levels of security. I try to make sure that anything I risk is in line with God's calling and gifting in my life. Then it becomes a measured or predictable risk, not just a crazy gamble.

I have mentioned that within nine months of my "born-again" experience God called me to ministry. You have to remember that I was a failing student, afraid of people, and almost flunked speech class. In short, I didn't have any of the native qualities that would seem so essential for ministry.

Yet God urged me to take one small step of risk after another. Each day as I began to read the Bible, I told God I was willing to follow his direction. As I read the Bible, the Holy Spirit caused certain words, phrases, and concepts to stand out. I incorporated these ideas into my daily thought life and actions. I began to think and act differently in many areas of my life. I had a growing confidence to take small risks in actions and responsibilities each day. After a number of years of measured risk-taking, I look back to see that I'm a very different person.

In my first student pastorate I was only responsible for the morning services. In the second small country church I was responsible for the morning services and the evening youth group.

Each step of risk through the years has expanded what I felt able to do.

Today I feel competent to speak to thousands of people, to work in cross-cultural situations through an interpreter, to administer a large local church, to run a doctoral program for a seminary, to appear on national radio or television, to write articles, booklets, and books, among other things.

The point is, I didn't get to this level of competency in one big step. It was through a number of small steps of risk that gradually expanded my level of competency.

It's also important to realize that risk, followed by success, not only increases competency but also changes our self-image to a broader, more positive view. Risk coupled with defeat tends to reverse the cycle. That's why it's so important to make sure that you are taking small risks in the direction of God's calling and gifting in your life. Following God is still a risk, but now it is predictable, with a high likelihood of success. Each new success will have the positive impact of increasing your sense of competence for future risks.

There's a cute story about a woodcarver who was carving a bear out of a block of wood. His young son saw him carving and was fascinated by the magnificent bear that was appearing. He asked his father if he could also have a block of wood.

The boy then hacked and chopped on his block until it was nothing but a pile of splinters. In confusion and disappointment he said to his father, "My piece of wood didn't have a bear in it."

The person who best knows how to carve the raw material of your life is God. We don't have the full vision of what we can become nor do we have the skill to transform ourselves. That's why I can't overemphasize your need to allow God to do that delicate process of forming you.

I believe that personally knowing God gives you the capacity to risk and the courage to change to become a special person. The following activities can speed your growth.

Individual Growth Activities

1. Add a few more items to the lists you started earlier in this chapter.
   - a. All the things I like to do:
   - b. All the things I am able to do:
   - c. The most negative influences, events, or people in my life:
   - d. The most positive influences, events, or people in my life:
   - e. I am most angry at . . .
   - f. I am most happy with . . .
   - g. Before I die I want to . . .
2. Identify items that seem to fit together in all the lists. For example: items that indicate you are an outdoor person, musical, or adventurous.
3. Plan to get involved in several of the items on your list of "all the things I like to do" that you are not currently doing.

Group Growth Activities

1. Each person can share three or four items from some of the lists that he or she feels comfortable to share.
2. Share patterns that you notice in your own life, or encourage the group to give their observations of patterns in your life.
3. All the members should commit themselves to begin a small thought or behavior change this next week that will bring their personal activities more in line with God's unique creation in them.

Chapter 6

Qualities That Build Friendships

What is friendship? Sometimes I'm surprised that someone calls me a friend when I may only have met this person one time.

Sometimes we refer to people at work, in the community, in our church or club as friends when really they're just acquaintances. Our relationship with them is casual and superficial.

When I use the word **friendship,** I'm thinking of a depth relationship that includes such things as support, understanding, acceptance, love, trust, and loyalty, among other qualities.

Friendship is costly. Personally it demands a lot of us in terms of giving ourselves and our time. Friendship is an investment. Friendship is also receiving—being nurtured, enriched, and strengthened by another person.

Now, let's focus on you and some of the qualities that you need to develop to make your friendships really work.

Nonjudgmental

A woman from a nearby town called me to talk about her marriage problems. At the end of the conversation, she said, "It was easy to talk to you. I wish my husband would come to see you." Then she added, "If he does come to talk to you, don't bawl him out for not being a better husband." Her comment fascinated me. She was grateful that I was not judgmental toward her, but not quite sure that I would be nonjudgmental with her husband.

It's common for people to be apprehensive as they start to share. They usually expect us to be judgmental. Sometimes they have good reason to fear, because we **are** judgmental. To be a friend, you must develop the quality of not censuring. Your friend should be able to tell you anything, to express all his or her feelings, both the acceptable and the ugly. That doesn't mean you won't ultimately help your friend seek a solution or change his or her lifestyle, but your response while the problem is being aired is not one of reproach.

Repeatedly, we detect this nonjudgmental quality in Jesus while he was on earth. The only people who received sharp words from him were the pious, hypocritical religious leaders who didn't seem to need God. He accepted people's problems as experiences needing understanding or solutions.

An example of Jesus' nonjudgmental attitude is found in John 8, which relates the incident of the woman caught in adultery. In John 4 Jesus cares for the Samaritan woman. Jesus expressed the same attitude as he hung on the cross and spoke to the repentant thief, "Today you'll be with me in paradise."[1]

Being a friend is not sitting as a judge behind a high desk looking down as your friend pathetically exposes his or her inner feelings to you. Friendship is sitting cross-legged on the floor on the same level as your friend, seeing through your friend's eyes, and nonjudgmentally understanding what your friend feels.

Accepting

Acceptance is a quality that proceeds logically as the next step after being nonjudgmental. If you are a person who always believes your viewpoint is the best, though, you will tend to be judgmental and not accept other people.

Myron D. Rush, author of *Richer Relationships,* has said, "Problems in relationships occur as a result of individuals being so committed to their own views, opinions, ideas, and feelings that they abuse or neglect those of others."[2]

The Bible puts it this way: "Do nothing out of selfish ambition or vain conceit, but in humility consider others better than yourselves. Each of you should look not only to your own interests, but also to the interests of others."[3]

Acceptance means that you are willing to set aside some of your normal viewpoints and, instead, value and appreciate the viewpoints of others and their uniqueness.

During a seminar, Dr. Paul Tournier, the great Swiss psychiatrist, said that people who came to study his counseling methods were often disappointed because "I have no methods. All I do is accept people."[4]

A Great Loss

Feeling accepted or rejected has influenced the direction of many lives and even of the world. Gandhi was one such person.

> Gandhi studied the New Testament with zeal and could quote from the Scriptures in a way that would put most Bible school students to shame. He once entertained the possibility of becoming a Christian, but there were several circumstances which turned him away from this decision.
>
> He had often seen the disparity between Christ and Christians. He said, "Stoning prophets and erecting churches to their memory afterwards has been the way of the world through the ages. Today we worship Christ, but the Christ in the flesh we crucified."

Gandhi lived in South Africa during the most formative period of his life, and a few nasty incidents there did little to disabuse him of his notions of Christianity. He encountered blatant discrimination in that ostensibly Christian society, being thrown off trains, excluded from hotels and restaurants, and made to feel unwelcome even in some Christian gatherings.

Gandhi graciously omits from his autobiography one more painful experience that occurred in South Africa. The Indian community especially admired a Christian named C. F. Andrews whom they themselves nicknamed "Christ's Faithful Apostle." Having heard so much about Andrews, Gandhi sought to hear him. But when C. F. Andrews was invited to speak in a church in South Africa, Gandhi was barred from the meeting—his skin color was not white.

Commenting on Gandhi's experiences in South Africa, E. Stanley Jones concludes, "Racialism has many sins to bear, but perhaps its worst sin was the obscuring of Christ in an hour when one of the greatest souls born of a woman was making his decision."[5]

Tony Campolo has said, "Who knows what impact Christianity might have had on India if the father of that nation had embraced our faith. Can it be that a Hindu understood the teachings of Jesus on love and power better than the theologians and preachers of the church of Christ? We will have to wait until Judgment Day for the answer to that question."[6]

Don't Throw the Toast

Haim Ginott, in his book *Between Parent and Child,* describes a situation from a parent discussion group where group members expressed the difference between being accepted and being rejected.

Leader: Suppose it is one of those mornings when everything seems to go wrong. The telephone rings, the baby cries, and before you know it, the toast is burnt. Your husband looks over the toaster and says: "My God! When will you learn to make toast?!" What is your reaction?

Mrs. A: I would throw the toast in his face!

Mrs. B: I would say, "Fix your own _____ toast!"

Mrs. C: I would be so hurt I could only cry.

Leader: What would your husband's words make you feel toward him?

Parents: Anger, hate, resentment.

Leader: Would it be easy for you to fix another batch of toast?

Mrs. A: Only if I could put some poison on it!

Leader: And when he left for work, would it be easy to clean up the house?

Mrs. A: No, the whole day would be ruined.

Leader: Suppose the situation is the same: the toast is burnt but your husband, looking over the situation, says, "Gee, honey, it's a rough morning for you—the baby, the phone, and now the toast."

Mrs. A: I would drop dead if my husband said that to me!

Mrs. B: I would feel wonderful!

Mrs. C: I would feel so good I would hug him and kiss him.

Leader: Why?—that baby is still crying and the toast is still burnt?

Parents: That wouldn't matter.

Leader: What would make the difference?

Mrs. B: You feel kind of grateful that he didn't criticize you—that he was with you, not against you.

Leader: And when your husband left for work, would it be difficult to clean up the house?

Mrs. C: No! I'd do it with a song.[7]

The difference in this illustration was, as Mrs. B says, she would feel that "he was with you, not against you." To be a real friend, your friend must feel accepted, that you are with him.

As you accept your friend, you allow the draining off of emotions. You give freedom to vent frustrations. The fact that you're able to accept and identify with your friend is often all that is needed to reduce the pressure inside.

Recently an emotionally shredded college student came to me. She had gone with a guy for three years, and now he was saying he wanted out. Sharon had been dumped two other times after long, deep relationships. I was sitting across our living room from her. As the story began to unfold, she started to cry. Her whole body convulsed in anguished sobs. I got up from the couch, crossed the room, and sat down on the floor at her feet. I put my hand on her hand and said, "It's okay."

After Sharon cried for a while, I said, "You may feel as if you're worthless, that no one will ever love you. You probably feel that somehow you've never learned to relate to people and that you'll be condemned to always be alone in the world." As I began to describe what I thought she was feeling from what I had learned by listening to her, she repeatedly nodded in agreement and said, "Yes, yes."

There was a sigh of relief. She was accepted. I understood her pain and fear. It didn't change the reality that she had just been dumped, but she was able to go on because she could honestly share with me her real feelings. As we prayed together, she also began to sense God's acceptance and love.

Genuineness

Being a friend means you are not phony. Your friend wants to know that the warm care you express is not a professionalism that you are putting on.

Paul Tournier in *The Adventure of Living* talks about the problem of becoming an impersonal professional in our relationships. He warns against developing habits or routines that are false. He tells the story of a woman whom he had been counseling. She seemed to be making good progress and on one occasion thanked him for his caring love. But then she questioned his genuineness with these words, "You are very kind, but don't you love all your patients in just the same way?"

Dr. Tournier responded by saying that her remark made him shudder. "Suppose love did become a 'job'! How horrible!"[8]

Being genuine is both an attitude you possess and a skill to be learned. In chapter 11, we'll look at the skill of being genuine.

Self-Disclosing

Your friend looks for reality in you. That person does not want to be treated as a patient but as a friend. Letting the other person get to know you through self-disclosure assures that person that you are genuine. True friendships are built on a broad base of understanding each other. As a person knows more about you, your friendship will deepen.

As a pastor in Urbana, Illinois, I frequently visited various small groups in our church, allowing them to ask me any questions they wanted. Most of their questions centered around me—what I liked to eat, when I learned to sail, what I read, and how I relaxed—rather than issues about the church or Christian living. After these sessions, people said they felt freer to relate to me because they had come to know me better. My pulpit and teaching ministry had more meaning, they said, because they now knew me as a person, not a preaching machine.

Allow your friends to get to know you in many areas of your life so that they can learn about your values, lifestyle, and goals. We'll talk more about the skill of self-disclosure in chapter 11.

Trusting

An article in *Psychology Today* entitled "Trust and Gullibility" shows that people who are "high trusters" are no less intelligent or more gullible than others. But "they are happier, more likable—and more trustworthy."[9]

If you want to be a true friend, you have to be able to keep confidences. Your friend must be able to trust in you and not be afraid that what has been shared will be known by everyone. If I asked you to name people you know who can't keep confidences, you could probably name several. Remember this axiom: He who has unhinged jaws has few friends.

Gossip is condemned in the Bible because it means breaking trust with a friend. It is taking unfair advantage of a friendship. The Bible categorizes it as a sin. (See Leviticus 19:16 and Proverbs 16:28.)

I have often laughed at one of my favorite stories about three preachers traveling together to a conference. As they traveled, they began to reveal their private sins. One minister said, "You know, I wouldn't want anybody else to know, but when I get away from my congregation, I really like to do a little heavy drinking. It makes me feel so good!" The second one felt encouraged to reveal his pet sin and said, "You know, it's funny, but when I get away from my parish where smoking is strictly forbidden, I like to relax a bit with a big cigar."

There was a long silence, and the first two men kept looking at the third preacher, wondering if he was going to share his secret sin. Finally, as they prodded him, he said, "Men, I really hate to tell you this, but my pet sin is gossip, and I can hardly wait to get home!"

If the basis of your friendship is to have juicy stories to share with others, your lack of confidentiality will soon isolate you from deep friendships.

Caring, Loving

Astoundingly, God, who created the universe, who has unlimited power and knowledge, who can stabilize galaxies in space or redirect a human thought pattern, is not described in his basic essence as "thought" or "power." Neither does he want us characterized that way.

The Bible says simply, "God is love."[10] Jesus' directive to his disciples was not power or concepts but love. Jesus said, "Love each other just as much as I love you. Your strong love for each other will prove to the world that you are My disciples"[11]

Think about it. "Love is the only true creative force in the world."[12]

Caring and love must be verbalized if you are going to be a friend. Certainly much of your care and love will be communicated by all the positive things you do for your friend. But your spoken expressions of care will build a strong bridge between the two of you.

At the same time, verbalizing your caring and love builds strengths within your friend. Your care gives your friend "love dollars" or a positive feeling about himself or herself, life in general, God, and you.

It's Okay to Show Love

Sometimes, as one of our daughters shares with us a struggle in her life, her face reveals a need for assurance. Sally and I may not have any solution to the problem. We may only listen, reflect back her comments, and accept her. But we have found that it is important to go a step further. We need to put our arms around our daughter, hold her close for a moment, and say, "We really love you, honey." The verbalizing of love and the expression of caring through a hug gives the needed assurance.

If your friend doesn't get assurance, then that friend inwardly asks if you really love him or her. Finally the friend is humiliated by having to ask you, "Do you really love me?" A friendship usually cools when someone is forced to ask, "Do you really care about me?" So watch for that look in your friend's eyes that signals, "I need assurance."

A few years ago Sally and I, along with Becki, our youngest daughter, visited our two older daughters at Taylor University in Indiana. It was parents' weekend. The five of us were sitting in the dorm lounge, talking. One of our girl's friends, Patty, had casually joined us.

We finished visiting, and before we left for home, I said, "Let's pray together." We reached out our hands to form a circle, including Patty with our family. When we finished, I noticed that everyone had a comfortable look—except Patty. She had that look that says, "I need somebody to tell me I'm important and worth loving." As we stood up, ready to go, I walked over to Patty and put my arms around her. She began to sob.

I learned that her mother and father had not come for that parents' weekend because they were separating from each other. She was feeling abandoned and wasn't sure anyone really loved her.

Being a friend means you watch for the look that says, "I need to know you care for me." Then verbalize your care in simple, direct form—"I care about you. You're important to me."

Committed

Being a friend is serious business. It's costly. Jesus put it this way, "Greater love has no one than this, that he lay down his life for his friends."[13] To be committed to a person in friendship means that you will love whether your friend is up or down, pleases or displeases you, or is a success or a failure.

Commitment in friendship restricts us from using people. We want nothing in return. We want only to bless. Commitment has a strong dimension of self-sacrifice. It is laying down our lives emotionally for our friends.

During college, as I mentioned, I had a close friendship with a group of guys. In the past few years I've come to realize that since that time I have been so busy "saving the world" I have almost forgotten those friends. These were men with whom I hitchhiked across the country, slept in fields, and shared food and money. We owned old cars together. We laughed, cried, and prayed together. We double- and triple-dated together. We saw God work the miracle of his blessing in each of our lives. And we all had a part in counseling each other about life, career, and marriage.

Because of busyness and geographical distance, I have failed these friends in my commitment. Recently I have been working at renewing these relationships, and it's been exciting to see these friendships, like smoldering fires, brought back to life again.

Commitment is an act of will that makes all the other friendship qualities work. Commitment is like the engine that enables your car to move. Your car might have a great stereo radio, wonderful seats and interior, new tires, and a great paint job, but without a motor, you really only have a beautiful hulk of metal. The motor makes it work.

Commitment is what you need in order to love and care when you don't feel like it. Commitment enables you to be trusted, to be consistent, to be genuine, to be accepting and nonjudgmental. Without commitment you probably won't pull off any of those other qualities. Without commitment you might find it easy to slip out the back door of a relationship when it gets tough.

Let's face it, there are times when it's not fun to be a friend. Commitment keeps you going, forgiving, and downplaying the negative in your friendship. Commitment keeps you moving and improving your friendship.

Forever Friend

"The commitment of love, at whatever level, has to be a permanent thing, a life-wager. If I say that I am your friend, I will always be your friend, not as long as or until anything. I will always be there for you. Effective love is not like the retractable point on a ballpoint pen."[14] These powerful words by John Powell have been a great influence on my thinking about quality friendships.

Don't plan on temporary friendships. Make them for keeps. Be committed to people forever. Obviously, you can't do this with every person you meet. But our mobile society is so busy with surface relationships that we never get around to the "forever commitments"—the kind where we are willing to extravagantly sacrifice ourselves for each other to create enduring friendships.

One of the most meaningful small groups I ever shared in lasted only two weeks. In those two weeks we went through feeling suspicious, fearful, competitive, and isolated before we finally broke through into a caring relationship in which we wanted the best for the other. By the end of those two weeks we had become brothers and true friends.

During that time I was going through deep trauma in my life. Our youngest daughter had recently had her left leg amputated above the knee. I felt that God had abandoned me. I didn't know whether I could ever preach or talk about God again. Two of the men in that group expressed real friendship commitment.

One said, "I am responsible for hiring personnel at the school where I work. If you don't feel you can continue in the pastorate, remember a job is always waiting for you there." The second said to me just before I flew home, "I am only a couple of hours away by air; if you need me, I'll be there."

That kind of "forever commitment" in friendship is significant and life changing. It's that kind of commitment that I have felt from my wife all through our marriage. She is committed to stand by me, no matter what kind of hell goes on inside or outside me. If you want to be a friend, then plan a "forever commitment"; be someone who will lay down his life for his friends.[15]

Enabling

A true friend calls out growth in the other person. You stimulate your friend. You are an enabler. Of course, you can't actually make anyone grow, but being a friend means you provide the stimulus that will promote growth.

Teachable moments occur in all our lives. But at other times our minds are like two-and-a-half pounds of hamburger. Nothing could happen, no matter how stimulating the situation might be. A friend recognizes the teachable moments in another's life and takes those opportunities to stimulate and enrich the friend's life.

Look for Teachable Moments

Deuteronomy 6 gives a directive for parents to teach their children about God: "And you shall teach them [the commandments] diligently to your sons and shall talk of them when you sit in your house and when you walk by the way and when you lie down and when you rise up."[16]

This verse describes the teachable moments that are a normal part of everyday life. You can encourage your friend's growth during casual moments through the day—in ordinary conversation, while sitting together, walking, riding in the car or on a bike, or eating. It can happen in the morning, at noon or night. The best growth happens during life's routine experiences.

Self-Revelation Helps

You can also draw out growth in your friend by revealing yourself. The gradual unveiling of your personality to another is much the same as peeling off leaves of lettuce. Your self-revelation helps your friend reveal himself or herself by talking about what is going on inside.

Small groups are a good place to model this gradual revealing and enabling process. After the members of a small group meet three or four times, they usually come to sort of a plateau. Up to this point the members may have been unconsciously jockeying for positions of leadership and recognition within the group. Usually not much has been risked or revealed.

But if someone discloses a bit about himself or herself, the group will probably move to deeper levels of sharing, trust, and caring. Or as in the lettuce illustration, the group moves closer to the center of the head—closer to each other.

Strong, Firm

A friend is also able to be firm. Friendship does not mean we are manipulated into acting against our moral standards or against what is best for our friend.

Ann Kiemel, in her book *I Love the Word Impossible,* speaks of the repeated hassles that came to her as a college administrator. One girl had wanted to live in a special dorm room. She already had curtains for it, but a senior who had priority chose the room. The girl came to Ann's office, very angry and pounding her fists on the desk. Ann listened to the verbal torrent of anger and then responded with gentle firmness. "Donna, I know how hurt and angry you must feel. I have felt those things lots of times too. I am really sorry. It is against my integrity to change something I think is very fair, but I give you every right to feel upset. I understand. It's okay."[17]

It's important that we not think of our friendship as an excuse for weakness when we know that firmness is the best for our friend. We are, after all, to be enablers.

As a college pastor, I was involved in thousands of hours of premarital counseling. I routinely told couples at the beginning of our sessions that I was not sure that I would marry them. If I, in good conscience, began to see that they were not going to succeed in marriage, I would encourage them to delay while they did further growing or even reconsidered whether to marry each other at all.

Encouraging a couple to delay a marriage is not a pleasant task. These students were my friends and I didn't enjoy disappointing them. But by being firm in premarital counseling, I may have been, in the long run, a better friend than if I had said, "Oh, well, these people are my friends; I can't let them down. I'll do what they want me to do. I'll perform the marriage."

Proverbs 17:17 says, "A friend loves at all times." Being a friend means you are willing to be firm, even when it's hard.

Spiritually Concerned

The essence of the human personality is spiritual. Deep friendships move beyond simple sharing of activities to understanding each other's spiritual core where values, guilt, aspiration, failure, and forgiveness reside.

A basic way you can touch the deepest level of your friend's life is through prayer. In Philippians 1:9–11 Paul prayed that five different areas of growth would be experienced by his friends in Philippi. An InterVarsity staff friend, Dave, showed me how this Scripture can be used to pray for a friend. Insert your friend's name in Paul's prayer (Philippians 1:9–11, *The Living Bible*). Instead of saying, "My prayer for you is that you will overflow more and more with love for others," change it to read, "God, my prayer for Bill is that he will overflow more and more with love for others."

Follow that same pattern through the rest of Paul's prayer. It's interesting to note that in many sections of the New Testament there are prayers where your friend's name could be inserted. (Another example is Ephesians 1:15–20.)

Improvement Not Perfection

As you think back over all of the qualities that we have just talked about, you may be saying to yourself, "Wow! I don't know if I can do all of that." You might feel as if you'll never develop all these qualities.

Remember, we're not shooting for perfection. What I want you to do is to review this chapter thinking about each of the ten qualities we've talked about. How would you rate yourself on a scale from 0 to 10? Remember, anything above "0" is positive.

Keep on doing the things you are already doing. Also take another look at these ten qualities and pick one trait you would like to focus intensely on for the next three or four weeks. Plan ways to help this trait grow in you.

Suppose you choose acceptance. Deliberately put yourself in the shoes of other people that you read about or hear about. Keep asking yourself, "What makes them tick? Why do they think that way? What are they feeling now?"

Keep on probing for answers and reasons until finally you realize that, if you experienced exactly what they are experiencing, you would probably react to life the same way they react. Now you're getting close to acceptance.

Maybe you will choose spiritual concern as the quality you want to develop. Focus on some of the suggestions in that section as you seriously pray for your friend's life and needs.

You've probably noticed that a number of these qualities also have a skill dimension. In the coming chapters we will focus on the skills that will help you to make deep and lasting friendships. But for now, scan over this chapter once more and think about the qualities needed for friendship.

Individual Growth Activities

1. Rate yourself in each of the ten qualities discussed. Circle the number that is most appropriate. (0 = needing lots of work; 10 = doing great.)

A. Nonjudgmental	0	1	2	3	4	5	6	7	8	9	10
B. Accepting	0	1	2	3	4	5	6	7	8	9	10
C. Genuine	0	1	2	3	4	5	6	7	8	9	10
D. Self-disclosing	0	1	2	3	4	5	6	7	8	9	10
E. Trusting	0	1	2	3	4	5	6	7	8	9	10
F. Caring/Loving	0	1	2	3	4	5	6	7	8	9	10
G. Committed	0	1	2	3	4	5	6	7	8	9	10
H. Enabling	0	1	2	3	4	5	6	7	8	9	10
I. Strong/Firm	0	1	2	3	4	5	6	7	8	9	10
J. Spiritually Concerned	0	1	2	3	4	5	6	7	8	9	10

2. What project ideas come to mind to strengthen your weakest areas? (Reread that section of the chapter to help you with specific projects.)

Group Growth Activities

1. Share with the group what you feel to be the one strongest quality in each member of the group.
2. Share what you feel to be **your** weakest friendship quality.
3. Help each other decide specifically how each person will work on his or her weakest trait during this next week. (Plan to report how you did at the next meeting.)

Part Three

SKILLS FOR DEEP AND LASTING FRIENDSHIPS

Chapter 7

Skill #1

Attending: Focusing on Your Friend

A few weeks ago I was having lunch with a couple to talk about their marriage problem. The story of agony, disappointment, and frustration poured out of the hurting husband. During Dan's most intense sharing of his hurt, his wife, Karen, reached into her purse, pulled out her fingernail clipper, and started to trim her nails.

I winced as I realized what she was communicating to her husband. Karen's actions were saying, "I'm not terribly interested in what you're saying."

Sometimes in a situation like this, the other person will say, "You're not listening." In this case, if Dan had said this aloud, Karen would have responded, "I'm hearing every word." In fact, she might have been able to repeat the words as effectively as a tape recorder. But her actions communicated that she didn't care.

Paying attention to another person is more than just having your ears turned on. Your whole body must be paying attention!

After what seemed like a long time, Karen put her fingernail clipper away, took out her emery board, and started to file her nails. I couldn't believe it. She continued to say by her body language, "I'm not listening. You're not important. My nails have a higher priority to me than you do."

Attending Is Focusing

Paying attention to someone is often referred to, in more technical language, as **attending.** As I chat with you about focusing on people, I'm going to use the word **attending** to mean that you are paying attention. **Attending** means that you are "with" your friend. It means that you have oriented yourself physically and psychologically toward your friend.

Attending is having your body squarely facing your friend and your mind undistracted. All of your physical and emotional attention is focused on this person. When you focus your body and your attention on the other person, you are saying, "I care for you; I am interested in what you say and who you are. I want to know more about you. You are important to me."

I want to caution you again. It is possible to use these friendship skills in a false way. It is absolutely crucial that you **not** use this skill to cultivate a friendship if you don't really care for the other person.

If you find yourself manipulating someone, then a few questions may help you to keep focused. Ask yourself, "Do I really care for this person? Am I nonjudgmental and genuine, or am I using this skill to manipulate this person for my own ends?" If you manipulate people because you're lonely and need friends, then you must work on developing a more positive self-image.

But now I'm assuming that you are learning to value yourself more and in all sincerity, you want to use your friendship skills to enrich the lives of others. Start by remembering that attending is focusing your body and mind on your friend.

Attending Is Looking

A mother was working at the kitchen sink while her little daughter played on the floor. The girl was building something and kept saying, "Mommy, look what I'm doing. See what I'm building. Look, Mommy." The mother would respond, "Yes, honey, that's nice," or "Um-hmm," but continued to peel the potatoes for supper. Finally the little girl pulled on her mother's skirt and said, "Mommy, look—look with your eyes!"

Attending is a simple concept. It involves focusing your attention through your body and mind on another person. It means giving eye contact. Gerard Egan, author of *The Skilled Helper,* reminds us, "People want more than physical presence in human communication; they want the other person to be fully there, meaning *psychological* or *social-emotional* presence."[1]

Looking at another person is one major way to communicate that you are fully there. Looks communicate your emotions. A look can be a warning, an expression of love, a put-down, or even a seductive message. Looking at your friend helps communicate that you are really tuning in.

Looking is also a way of collecting information. Your friend may be giving facial expressions that show a fear of not being accepted, or happiness, pain, worry, or appreciation and affirmation of you. If you are not looking, you will only pick up a small percentage of what your friend is communicating.

Attending Is Nonverbal

Studies show that much of the message we give or receive is in nonverbal form. Think about these percentages which show how we communicate messages:

- 7 percent is verbal, through the words themselves
- 38 percent is vocal, through the tone or inflection of our voice

- 58 percent is through our facial expression which tells our feelings behind the words.

In the book *Silent Messages,* Albert Mehrabian says, "Thus, the impact of facial expression is greatest, then the impact of the tone of the voice (or vocal expression), and finally that of the words. If the facial expression is inconsistent with the words, the degree of liking conveyed by the facial expression will dominate and determine the impact of the total message"[2]

A number of studies show that women tend to look at people more during a conversation, regardless of who is speaking. Other studies show that both sexes experienced "the most discomfort when they were speaking and their partner wasn't looking at them. Such a finding implies that looking while listening is more important to the interaction than looking while speaking."[3]

Attending must not be taken lightly. It cannot be an option for friendship. It is a powerful force that will affect your relationships.

If you want your relationship to flourish and be stimulating, be attentive when your friend speaks. Some interesting dynamics will take place, as shown by the following experiment.

At a prearranged signal, six students in a psychology seminar switched from the traditional student's slouched posture of passive listening, to attentive posture and active eye contact with the teacher. During the non-attending condition, the teacher lectured from his notes in a monotone, using no gestures, and paying little or no attention to the students. However, once the students began to attend, the teacher began to gesture, his verbal rate increased, and a lively classroom session was born.

At another prearranged signal later in the class, the students stopped attending and returned to the typical passive student posture and participation. The teacher, after some painful seeking for continued reinforcement, returned to the unengaging teacher behavior with which he had begun the class. . . . Simple attending changed the whole picture.[4]

Attending Is Both Positive and Negative

You probably have experienced both positive and negative attending from other people. For a moment, focus on your experiences and ask how you measure up in this skill.

Positive attending is shown by such expressions as:

• a warm smile
• an enthusiastic handshake
• a wave
• leaning forward in the chair
• turning to face someone more completely
• opening a door
• assisting with a chair
• a touch on the shoulder
• a hug
• a kiss
• sliding a chair up closer
• taking off sunglasses

Most people think of these actions as positive and most people feel closer to the person who does these things on their behalf.

On the other hand, the following are emotional turn-offs for most people:

• a frown
• a glare
• gradually stepping back
• silence with no body reaction
• turning the body slightly away
• looking at your belt buckle while someone is talking
• looking over your shoulder

- glancing at your watch
- drumming your fingers
- yawning
- sighing

These negative acts cause people to think you are not interested in them. Most people feel awkward and report a degree of personal inadequacy when these negative behaviors are expressed toward them.

I'm a professional people watcher. When I'm with someone, I watch the whole body to pick up clues. That person's body fills in some of the blanks in what is being said.

Sometimes being sensitive to what people are saying can become painful. When I was a pastor, I struggled with being finished preaching at twelve o'clock. People teased me about being long-winded. I always laughed it off, but when everyone's watch alarm started to go off—beep-beep-beep, **beep-beep,** beep-beep, bzzz—I knew the people were telling me something even though they sat there smiling pleasantly.

What bothered me most during the symphony of beeps was when people looked at their watches, nodded in puzzlement, raised their wrists to their ears, and shook their watches. It appeared as if I had now become so boring to them that time was absolutely standing still. These same patient saints would greet me after the service and say, "That really was a great message." Their words and their watches were not giving me the same message.

You will have a strong positive impact on your friends as you pay attention to them. But remember to make your words, facial expressions, and tone all match. As I mentioned earlier, looking at a person, focusing your eyes on that person, and leaning your body forward are powerful aspects of attending.

Attending Is Physical Presence

Most people experience some crises, such as death, divorce, loss of a job, or a major disappointment. At such times, the people I pastored said they most appreciated my physical presence with them. Yes, the people appreciated my love and care, but my presence was a strong stabilizing factor to them. Don't overlook the simple fact of "just being there" with your friend.

Your physical presence invites the other person to trust you, to open up, and to share with you. Friendship is built on a gradual revelation and sharing of two lives with common interests, goals, and aspirations.

Physical presence is a strong reinforcer. As you spend time with your friend, you are building that person's self-image. You are helping that person grow. It is an affirmation that says, "You are important to me."

The Attending Skill

An acronym to summarize the attending skill is used by Gerard Egan in *The Skilled Helper.* It's the word **SOLER.** Let's use this word and its symbolism to help you see what you need to do to accurately attend to your friend.

S – Squarely face your friend. "In North American culture facing another person 'squarely' is often considered a basic posture of involvement. It usually says, 'I am available to you; I choose to be with you.'"[5]

Even when people are seated in a circle, you will frequently see them turn their bodies toward the person to whom they are speaking. If your body is turned away from squarely facing the other person, you are communicating a lack of interest.

O – Open posture. Folding your arms, crossing your legs, and clenching your fists are all indications of a lack of interest and involvement in the other person. The reason, Egan points out, is that "an open posture is generally seen as non-defensive."[6]

If you go into your boss's office to ask for a raise, but he crosses his arms, leans back in his chair, and says, "Now what did you want to talk about," you will likely feel that he has decided not to listen—and you are probably right. When talking with a friend, let your arms and hands be relaxed and open. This position communicates your willingness to listen and care.

L – Lean toward your friend. It's interesting to watch people in a restaurant. You'll notice husbands and wives who are not really interested in each other, but who are together because it's their duty. They lean away from each other, they don't look at each other, and their bodies may not be facing each other.

In contrast, notice a dating couple. They lean toward each other, hanging on every word. They exchange every morsel of information and affection in this electric relationship. At the same time, their entire bodies communicate warmth, acceptance, and love.

Egan reminds us, "In North American culture, a slight inclination toward a person is often interpreted as saying, 'I am with you; I'm interested in you and in what you have to say.'"[7] Leaning back, with your legs and arms crossed communicates that "I'm not with you; you bore me."

On the other hand, leaning too far forward may intrude on the other person's private space and it may communicate that you are pushy. I remember one particular college girl who felt close to me when I was pastoring in Urbana. She usually stood about eighteen inches from me when we talked. I felt uncomfortable at that distance because my glasses focused at about three feet. So I would gradually move back. As a result, each Sunday morning she would back me across the foyer until I finally hit the wall, unable to escape.

Unfortunately, I was communicating to her that she was not

important. What I meant to communicate was that she was important, but my eyes could focus better on her if she were about thirty-six inches away. (Frequently I take off my glasses when I'm talking to people who want a shorter distance.)

Don't press in too closely. Appropriate leaning forward and facing friends squarely, however, does communicate that you are interested in them.

E – Eye contact. Eye contact is not staring. Maintaining eye contact doesn't mean that you look into a person's eyes all of the time. It's okay to look away. But it's crucial when the other person is speaking to look at him or her. Let your eyes move gently around your friend's face rather than staring that person down.

Some years ago I had a pastor friend who had read somewhere that if you don't look at people while they are talking, it indicates insecurity (which is essentially true). To make sure no one knew how insecure he was, he would stare unblinkingly at everybody to whom he talked. He would get a fixed bead on the bridge of your nose and stare at that spot relentlessly in a penetrating, unflinching, terrorizing stare. His eyes would become as big as saucers as he tried not to blink. I had the deepest desire to poke my finger in his eye just to see if I could make him blink. I also had trouble concentrating on the conversation because I was thinking about his piercing stare.

Good eye contact is not staring but gently moving your gaze over a person's face. Again Egan observes, "In North American culture fairly steady eye contact is not unnatural for people deep in conversation."[8] Maintaining a frequent eye contact with your friend says, "I'm with you. I like you. I want to hear what you're saying. You're important to me."

If you find yourself frequently looking away, it may be that you are reluctant to be with this person. Maybe this isn't the person on whom you ought to spend your friendship energy. Or it may indicate that you have a degree of discomfort in being this emotionally close or this intense with any friend.

R – Relaxed. Your body should be at ease, especially your face. If you're biting your lip, clenching your teeth, or squinting, your tenseness may indicate to your friend that you would rather be doing something else.

When I encourage you to be relaxed, I'm not asking you to violate any of the other concepts we have listed here under the **SOLER** acronym.

A negative illustration of being too relaxed was shown in a videotaping of a small-group session. "One of the participants was slouched down in his chair, his legs stretched out in front of him. Another member asked him how he liked the group experience. He seemed to be caught somewhat unaware and answered, hesitantly, that he had 'really enjoyed' the sessions.

"During the replay, when this part of the tape was played, he cried out, 'Turn it off! What a liar I am!' His whole body had cried out the real message."[9] The idea is to make sure that your body is telling the truth about your desire to build a friendship with this person.

I remember one University of Illinois student who talked to me about his deep desire to develop friendships. Pathetically, Tom asked, "Why don't people like me? Why can't I get close to people?" Even as he was talking to me, he was turned sideways, looking down at the floor, and fidgeting with a pencil. I suspected that frequently his body communicated an uneasiness to the very people he was trying to befriend.

This doctoral student, although quite advanced in his field of study, was undeveloped in his friendship skills. In fact, his bodily actions accurately portrayed his fear of people and his insecurity.

We worked on Tom's self-esteem, friendship attitudes, and the qualities of a maturing person (similar to the ideas we looked at earlier in this book). He began to develop a deeper understanding of himself, of God's love for him, and of his importance to other people. As a result, Tom began to rethink his research career. In fact, he changed so much that his research in biochemistry no longer interested him. He started dating regularly and later took a people-oriented job.

Attending Develops Through Sensitization and Practice

Your attending skills can rapidly develop as you notice other people's attending skills. Watch how other people carry out the attending skills that we spoke about under the acronym **SOLER**. At the same time, read your emotions as those people relate to you.

How do you feel when a person looks directly at you, nods, smiles, and says, "Uh-huh, uh-huh"? Probably you feel good! But how do you feel if someone frequently glances over your shoulder or at his or her watch? That person says, "Uh-huh, uh-huh," but is as expressionless as the stone faces carved on Mount Rushmore.

Sensitizing yourself by watching others and noticing your reactions will help you become a better attender. The following is a partial list of actions to notice as you watch the attending skills of other people. Ask yourself, "What reactions do I feel when other people attend to me in the following ways?"

- nodding the head
- slight smile
- quivering lower lip
- loud, quiet, or monotonous voice
- eyes wide open, squinting, or furtive glances
- sighs, yawns, or rapid breathing
- sitting upright
- wringing hands
- holding onto the chair

- blushing, turning pale
- arms crossed
- slouching in the chair

As you look at this list, try not to give only one interpretation for each thing that is happening. For example, a person in love might shake his or her head back and forth and say, "I don't believe you. You are just too good to be true." Moving the head back and forth doesn't always mean "no"; it can be a strong affirmation. Watch for several body signs before you draw any conclusions.

Remember, the purpose of this practice is not to help you "out-psych" other people. Rather, it is to encourage your own development so that you are a better attender.

Attending Over the Phone

One other caution. Remember to attend to people even when you are not physically with them. For example, during telephone conversations people will frequently ignore the other person with their body and believe that only the words are important.

Have you ever tried to talk over the phone to someone who is eating, doing dishes, brushing teeth, or working out? It's easy to have the feeling that the other person doesn't care.

Some people think since you can't see them doing the dishes you don't know they aren't paying attention. It's back to the old line, "I hear what you say," but, in fact, the person is partially distracted and misses a lot of the subtleties that are being communicated over the phone.

Hey, I'm guilty of this, too. If I take a phone call in my office, I frequently keep working at my desk while I talk to the other person. It's a bad habit.

Let's Review

• Attending is not for manipulation; rather, it is to assure a person that you do want to relate as a friend.

• Attending is a genuine expression only as you bring with it your caring qualities and positive self-image that we have talked about in earlier chapters.

• Attending does not mean that you become slavishly preoccupied with your body; rather, through sensitivity, you learn instinctively to be in tune with yourself and your body so that you are communicating love and care.

As we work through the book, you are probably noticing that each activity to improve your friendship skills will also help the other skills to develop. For example, in the next chapter we'll think about "creative listening." If you learn to listen effectively, you will automatically become a better attender. In later chapters we will talk about other skills that will help you to listen better as well as to be a better attender.

So hang in there. Practice each skill and attitude. Then see what God does in your personal life.

Following are some suggestions for individual and group use to develop attending skills.

Individual Growth Activities

1. Review the main ideas of this chapter. Identify which aspects of your attending skill are coming along well and which parts need work.
2. Identify people each day for the next week on whom you are going to "practice." Use one aspect of the attending skill and carefully watch their reactions to you. Remember: They are not to know that you are practicing. The goal is to practice enough so that your skills are natural and unnoticed.

Group Growth Activities

Divide into groups of three. One person should share about a friendship experience, another should use the attending skills, and the third should observe the first two. The observer should take notes and later give encouragement by identifying the positive expressions of the attending skills that were used. Rotate positions so that each person in the group gets to practice the attending skills.

Chapter 8

Skill #2

Listening: One Part of Communication

Two psychiatrists had their offices in the same building—one on the fifth floor, the other on the ninth. They also carpooled together. Each day they rode up the elevator together, the first getting off at the fifth floor, the second at the ninth. At the end of the day the ninth-floor psychiatrist would get on the elevator, meet his friend at the fifth floor, and together they would ride the elevator to the parking level and travel home.

Day after day the fellow from the fifth floor noticed how strong and refreshed his ninth-floor psychiatrist friend looked after working all day. After weeks of searching for an answer, he finally confronted his friend. "Why is it? We both come to work equally eager for the day's clients. At the end of the day, I am thoroughly drained, but you look as refreshed as at the beginning. Doesn't it exhaust you to listen to all those problems?" The ninth-floor psychiatrist smiled and shrugged, "Who listens?"

That's a sick joke, because we expect counselors genuinely to listen, but it does demonstrate the reality that many people don't. It also shows that listening is not a passive, relaxed activity. True listening (I will refer to it as **creative listening**) demands a great deal of emotional and physical energy.

Listening is not an option. It is essential for good relationships—essential to help your friend develop as a whole person and essential for your own personal development.

Paul Tournier has said, "No one can develop freely in this world and find a full life without feeling understood by at least one person. No one comes to know himself through introspection, or in the solitude of his own personal diary. Rather, it is in dialogue, in his meeting with other persons."[1]

What Is Creative Listening?

Most people need time to let their feelings bubble to the surface. They also need time to test you—to see if you are really a caring person. Creative listening gives your friend the permission to explore his or her feelings. At the same time, your willingness to listen creatively will give your friend the opportunity to see that you do care.

Your friend will send up a few trial balloons to see how well you listen. If you respond with true creative listening, that person will then trust you with more feelings and more personal information.

Not every conversation requires creative listening. Sometimes you will just laugh and chatter or visit about "what's happening" in your lives. The focus of this chapter, however, is to teach you how to use your creative listening skill at appropriate times to deepen your friendship.

Not Conversation

Creative listening does not mean that you are waiting for the other person to finish talking so that you can talk. Creative listening does not mean that you analyze what your friend says so that you can win an argument. Nor does this kind of listening mean that you wait for the opportunity to drop some great gem of truth on that person.

Creative listening draws the other person out so that he or she feels free to share. A night-and-day difference exists between hearing someone and listening. Do you remember that Jesus said, "They hear, but don't understand; they look, but don't see!"[2] It wasn't that the people in Jesus' day were unable to hear sounds with their ears. The problem was that they had no understanding.

Focus on Me!

Just this morning, while taking a little mini-break from writing this book, I went down to the kitchen. Sally was there and said, "I'm glad I could catch you. I want to tell you something about Fred, who's in the hospital."

I mumbled "Uh-huh" as I sat down at the table and started to edit some material the secretary had just typed. Sally quietly but emphatically spoke again: "I'm not going to tell you about Fred until I have your focused attention. I want you **really** to hear me."

She wasn't questioning the ability of my ears to hear. She was questioning my willingness to understand and feel her concern since I was preoccupied with editing.

Now you understand how listening ties in to attending. You can't really listen to another person until you focus your body, your personality, and your mind on that person and what your friend is trying to share.

Listening Problems

Following are six common areas that may cause you to be an ineffective listener.

Words. David Augsburger points out, "600,000 words are available in the English language. Of these, an educated adult uses

about 2,000. The most used 500 [words] have, according to
standard dictionaries, 14,000 different definitions. Each common
word must be used to cover a wide range of 'meanings.' This
pitifully small number of symbols must describe the infinite
richness of your and my experiences."[3]

Sometimes your comprehension of a word may get in the way
of listening effectively to your friend if you don't understand
exactly what that friend means by the words used. If you are
unclear about what your friend means, ask for clarification.

Screens. Each of us automatically blocks out certain sounds,
sights, smells, and sensations. Because of your screening mechan-
isms, your friend's thoughts may not be understood as your friend
intended.

The average American is bombarded with over four hundred
sales pitches a day. Our selective screens protect us from this
onslaught. What if you did everything you were told to do by each
advertiser that speaks to you through radio, TV, newspapers,
magazines, and billboards? You would be driven insane in one
day. You've learned to handle that kind of advertising nonsense
by tuning it out.

I've been told that during the Super Bowl in January 1986,
the TV network that broadcast the game declared a minute of
silence so that everybody could leave the TV to get a drink or go
to the bathroom. Think about that! Can you imagine how many
sewer lines were flowing at absolute capacity when all of the
toilets in the United States flushed within that one-minute period
of time? It's a wonder that the sewage treatment plants were not
washed completely off their foundations by the sudden rush of
water.

The broadcasters realized that people leave the TV sets
during ads so their decision was to "join 'em rather than fight
'em." Rather than have people miss the ads, they just didn't run
any during that minute.

You may do the same with your friend as we all do with TV ads. You may be only selectively hearing. Your screens may block out important information and feelings from your friend.

Suppose your friend is talking about a recent struggle in facing his or her father's death. If you've lost your own father, you may find yourself screening out your friend's feelings because they bring back too much pain to you.

Hot Buttons. Watch for "trigger" or emotion words. Following is a list of words that trigger explosive emotions in some people. I want you to allow these words to test your emotions.

- yuppie
- woman's libber
- damn it!
- sexy
- abortion
- homosexual
- women ministers
- incest

Did you feel any emotions as you read those words? Sometimes the trigger word goes off inside us like an explosion and distracts us from hearing what our friend is trying to say. If your friend uses a trigger word, deliberately calm yourself by inwardly thinking, "It's important not to be distracted from what my friend is saying because a word was used that happens to be a hot button with me."

Fatigue. Weariness can be another listening problem. A number of times my mind has shut off while someone is sharing with me. Other times I've actually fallen asleep and the other person has had to wake me up.

That's embarrassing to me—but think how humiliating and degrading it is to the other person! When trusted with a problem, I let that person down. If you are so exhausted you can't listen effectively, it would be better to say, "I really want to hear you because you are important to me, but I am so fatigued right now that I can't effectively tune in. Could we get together later?"

Answers. Another blockage to listening is our preoccupation with answers. Frequently, we listen to others only long enough to detect a problem. As soon as a problem is identified, we switch into a problem-solving mode and give all of our wonderful solutions.

Creative listening does not demand that you give answers. In fact, answers disrupt the listening process. Forget answers. Just carefully hear and understand the depths of the concerns your friend shares.

You'll be surprised how frequently a friend will say to you after a good creative listening session, "Boy, you really helped me." In reality, you may not have given any answers. Your help was in the form of listening and caring. You freed your friend to think about solutions and new directions.

Motivation. Perhaps the biggest problem with listening is motivation. Why are you listening? If you use listening skills to get friends, it's the wrong motive. If you listen to satisfy your own ego, that is, if you are elated because someone trusted you enough to share something personal, that's the wrong motive. If you listen to have some juicy tidbit to share with someone else, obviously, that's the wrong motive.

Creative listening is a skill that allows your friend to share with you as deeply as he or she cares to. It is a relational tool that enables your friend to grow and become all that person can be as God's special creation. The focus is always on your friend, never on you.

How to Listen

Dr. Vernon Grounds, president emeritus of Denver Seminary, taught me how to listen. For one of his classes our assignment was to listen to someone. We were to provide a climate so that a person could express his or her inner need. Rather than voicing our own thoughts or opinions, we were to draw a person out so that only what that person wanted to say would be said.

At the time, I was paying my seminary expenses by teaching people how to drive for the American Automobile Association. During one session I had a mid-life woman who was about halfway through her training program. It was the first time she had been scheduled with me, so I had never seen her before.

Since my seminary assignment on listening was due, I decided that she would be my "target." As usual, I had put this assignment off to the very last day. I had thoroughly convinced myself that I would not be able to do the assignment because I wasn't a counselor, I didn't have people coming to see me, and I didn't have an office. Besides, I really didn't believe that anyone would actually share anything if I used this dumb method.

The Target

In spite of my reservations and because I had to turn in the report, I decided that this woman would be the one to whom I would really listen. At first we talked about ordinary pleasantries—"Nice day today," and so on. I assured her she was doing a good job of driving. Then I asked, "Well, how has the day been going for you?" She hesitantly replied, "Well, okay, I guess." I could tell by the tone of her voice that "okay" didn't mean good.

Now pay close attention, because the typical response to that kind of comment would be to insert some of my own ideas. I could have said, "Yeah, I have okay days, too." If I had said that, I would have cut off the flow of feelings she was expressing and she probably would have changed the subject back to driving.

Creative listening means that you allow your friend to direct the flow of thoughts on any path. Listening is not conversation where each person shares equally. Listening creatively is a process in which you allow the other person to talk freely about his or her concerns. Your only task is to draw your friend out by continually giving permission to speak.

Instead of saying that I also had okay days, I did what Dr. Grounds had taught us. I tried to draw her out at the point of her last remark. So after she said, "Well, okay, I guess," I responded with, "Things aren't going too well today, huh?" I gave her the opportunity to stay on the subject. I subtly implied, "I'm willing to listen if you want to talk more."

She responded, "No, I guess not." Then there was a pause. I didn't fill the gap with my words of wisdom. I just waited for her to speak. Then she said, "It's my husband."

Permission to Talk

I didn't know what she meant by that, but I wanted to grant her the chance to continue talking, so I chose a rather general response and said, "Things aren't going so well with your husband?" (You see, it could have been his job, something between them, or an illness.) She filled the gap when I was quiet and allowed her to continue talking.

"We've been fighting a lot lately," she said. Again I waited and let her think. Then she added, "We argue a lot about his mother, who lives with us."

I carefully tried not to change the subject or insert any kind of suggestions, personal experience, or insights. I simply rephrased and reflected back what she had said to me. I said, "You and your husband argue a lot about your mother-in-law?"

"Yes," she said. "It always centers around the way my mother-in-law runs the house when I'm off at work."

It All Pours Out

From this point on I hardly needed to reflect back or say anything. She believed I wanted to listen to her and cared about what was happening. It was as if the dam had broken.

She poured it all out. I had just met this woman. I was with her only fifty minutes. Yet during that time I learned that she and her husband were having marital problems that were affecting their sex life. I learned that they fought about the mother-in-law living in the home and that my student deeply resented her mother-in-law teaching their little daughter to call the mother-in-law "Mommy" and to call my student, the actual mother, by her first name.

She further resented the fact that her husband never stood up for her. The mother-in-law ran the household and their private and family lives. They could never be alone as a couple or as a family of three. They always had to include the mother-in-law.

My student was frantic. She was considering running away from the family and divorcing her husband. She was experiencing self-condemnation and guilt. She didn't know where to turn or what to do.

When we came to the end of the driving lesson fifty minutes later, she turned to me with a rather puzzled look and said, "I don't know why I've told you all of this. I don't even know you. But I'm glad that you listened to me. It's been helpful just to have someone to talk to."

She knew that most of the driving instructors were students, so she asked me what I was studying to be. I told her I was planning to be a minister. Her response caught me off guard. She exclaimed, "Well, you'll make a _____ good minister!"

All I did was listen. I listened and repeatedly drew her out. In those few minutes, a whole new world of relating opened up to me. I came to see that if I really was to be a friend to people, I had to practice listening creatively.

What to Listen For

Remember, much of what you'll pick up from your friend will come from sources other than words. Continue to focus on the feelings of your friend. Listen for the unspoken fears. Ask yourself, "What makes my friend happy or sad?" "What does he like and dislike?"

Let's sum up some of the special areas where your sixth sense of listening needs to operate.

Listen for the nonverbals. What is your friend saying by what is not said? What are the feelings or ideas between the lines indicated by facial expressions or body movements? What words or ideas cause your friend to sigh? To look away?

Listen for ideas and information. Keep asking yourself, "How do the facts my friend is stating help me understand her so that I'm in a better position to care?"

Listen for evasiveness and gaps. For example, does your friend avoid talking about his father while freely discussing all of the other family members?

Listen for repeated phrases. If your friend says, "I don't know; I just don't know," it may indicate more than a lack of knowledge. It may be a sign of frustration with life, some degree of depression or insecurity. Creative listening pushes you to listen to the person behind the words—to hear with full intensity the feelings beneath the words.

Strengthening Your Listening Skills

Creative listening takes practice and discipline. As soon as your friend begins to share a problem, it may be your natural instinct to jump into a conversational mode either by sharing good advice or by sharing a similar problem. To be a friend you must use creative listening.

Creative listening requires a willingness to piece together bits of information. You hear your friend's words, but you also tune in on your friend's choice of words, tone of voice, various facial expressions, and body movements. In addition, creative listening means that you draw insights from your past understanding of this person as well as yourself, other human beings, and God.

Cautious questioning will assist you to be a better creative listener. The purpose of a question is not primarily for you to gather information; it is to assist your friend to continue talking.

Your friend might say, "You know, I was really lonely at the house last night." A poor response question would be, "Where was the rest of your family?" Your friend may not want to talk about where the family was. But your friend does want to talk about feelings of loneliness.

Another poor response might be, "Why do you think you are lonely all the time?" That question requires your friend to make an evaluation. In the early stages of sharing feelings, your friend needs you to listen and allow him or her to dump out feelings rather than to stop and analyze what's going on. That question might be very helpful later on after all the feelings about loneliness have come out.

A better response might be, "So, you were really feeling lonely last night?" Then your friend can carry the discussion any way he or she wants—about personal loneliness, a loss, or a family problem.

Good questions should build on the immediate ideas that have been shared by your friend. Good questions are the kind that cannot easily be answered with yes or no. For example, if you asked, "Were you lonely last night?" your friend could simply respond, "Yes," and it might be hard to get him or her started sharing again.

If your friend stops sharing and asks you a question, practice answering with a question of your own. Your friend might ask, "Do you think something is wrong with me because I'm lonely all the time?" You are being asked to analyze the situation. It might be better for your friend to continue to share more feelings. You could respond by asking, "What are your feelings when you use the words 'lonely all the time'?" Redirecting the conversation back to your friend allows the flow of sharing to continue.

Obviously, you want to avoid questions that would attack or put your friend down, such as, "Don't you think that was a stupid way to feel? Why can't you grow up and just start trusting God?"

Creative listening requires you to stop what you're doing and pay attention to people. Listening, to be effective, requires a relationship, a commitment on your part to be involved with this human being. Listening requires a commitment to attend, to tune in to the whole personality of your friend.

Jesus was always willing to stop and pay attention to individuals—even in the middle of a crowd. A blind man called out. Jesus stopped and focused on his need. A woman touched the hem of his garment. Jesus, sensing her presence and her faith, stopped and asked, "Who touched me?"[4] This incident interrupted him on his way to raise Jairus's daughter from death. Again and again Jesus stopped and gave focused attention to people. He was willing to allow his schedule to be disrupted so that he could minister to people.

One of my problems is that I don't like my plans disturbed. Maybe you're like me. The result is that we won't listen to people as we could, and that's bad for them and us. Isn't it funny that we draw comfort from the fact that God is interested in listening to us anytime? Yet we don't easily do that for others. The Lord stops what he's doing to pay attention to us. Repeatedly, Jesus demonstrated that "he is neither too busy, nor too popular to stop and listen."[5]

In *The Counselling of Jesus,* Duncan Buchanan reminds us, "Stopping is essential to listening. . . . It can be anywhere and anytime. When the person tugs your sleeve, for God's sake, stop and listen with all the resources God has given you."[6]

Results of Good Listening

Creative listening is an affirmation of the other person. Your friend will think, "Someone in this wide universe thinks I'm significant enough to give me concentrated attention. That feels good."

Another result of creative listening is that your friend is free to listen to his or her own feelings and words. Being seriously listened to gives a person a new objective view of the whole situation.

The serendipitous result of creative listening is that your friend is drawn closer to you, values your friendship, and is grateful that you care.

As you listen to your friend, a period of quiet will come when that person is talked out and feels that you understand the concerns. When that happens, your friend will probably want to listen to your counsel, observations, and insights. If you had tried to give insights earlier, your friend would not have heard them because of being preoccupied with the intensity of the immediate problem.

Creative listening will definitely change your life. As you deeply and intensely understand other human beings, you will become a more sensitive and caring person. You will also discover, as you practice the listening skill, that it will be easier for you to attend to people, to talk to them, to be empathetic, and vulnerable.

Listening is a major skill through which you can become an important person to yourself and a significant friend to other people.

Remind yourself that you're not shooting for perfection in

each of these skill areas. Any improvement in listening will also help all of the other areas to improve. So work on the activities described below and watch your life continue to change.

Individual Growth Activities

Practice your creative listening skill on several of the following people:

- a person younger than you
- a person older than you
- someone at work
- a person of another race
- someone of the opposite sex
- a poor person
- a powerful person
- a retired person

As you think about people to listen to, ask yourself, "Who could really use some encouragement by being listened to creatively?"

Group Growth Activities

1. Divide into groups of three. One person should share for about ten minutes, a second person should practice the listening skills, and the third should observe and give feedback on the positive parts of the session. Rotate positions so that each person has an opportunity to experience each part.
2. Commit yourself to listen creatively this coming week to at least one person. Ask the group to hold you accountable for giving feedback next week on how it went.

Chapter 9

Skill #3

Talking: Another Part of Communication

Frequently I've noticed that people who have trouble developing friendships not only need to learn how to listen but also how to talk. They need to learn how to carry on a dialogue.

A friendship, or peer relationship, is not just one person talking while the other listens. If one person is always the listener, you actually have more of a counseling situation than a friendship.

In a healthy relationship both people talk and share their true feelings, and both listen. A satisfying friendship, including marriage, involves equality in both talking and listening. The point to remember is that, as Reuel Howe says, "To whatever degree one part of the dialogue is lost, to that degree the relationship ceases to exist."[1]

In this chapter I'll push you to improve your talking skills so that you develop a flourishing relationship and have true dialogue with your friends.

Why Talk?

When I first dictated this chapter, I assumed that everyone wanted to talk. But after Sally read the manuscript, she reminded me that many people don't want to talk, don't know what to say, or believe they don't need to talk. So perhaps the first subject we need to tackle is "why talk?"

There's a basic human understanding about silence. If a person does not speak during a conversation, discussion, or dialogue, it is viewed as negative. For example, if a group of people are talking about where they'd like to eat dinner and everyone makes suggestions except Harry, the group will begin to prod Harry for his contribution.

If he says nothing, someone in the group is likely to say, "Harry, you don't ever want to do anything. You're a drag." The group members have decided, because Harry has not responded, that he must not want to go out to eat or doesn't want to be with the group. They've decided he is a party pooper. Their decision may not be accurate at all.

The point to remember, however, is that when you are in a conversation or discussion, you must join in or you will be increasingly suspected of disagreeable motives and intentions. You may eventually be isolated from the group.

Why People Don't Talk

Sometimes it's helpful to understand the negative part of a topic so that we can make positive corrections. I've spent thousands of hours in counseling sessions listening to various human relational problems. In the area of not talking, I notice three major reasons why people don't talk.

1. They don't know what to say. Sometimes nontalkers confess, "I just don't know what to say in a conversation." Here are a few common reasons why nontalkers don't know what to say.

- **Uninformed.** Nontalkers may not be keeping up on current events and items of interest to the people with whom they are in touch.
- **Insensitive to people and their needs.** People with an underdeveloped sense of empathy have less to talk about because they don't feel human needs.
- **Insecure.** People who feel uncomfortable with themselves or their own ideas may not take the risk of talking.
- **Resistant.** A person may say, "I don't know what to say," when in reality he or she may not feel comfortable with the person or the process. In addition, that person may feel powerless to change the situation. The only recourse is a passive resistance that results in silence.

2. They know what to say, but don't care. Sometimes a nontalker is not an uninformed person or insensitive, insecure, or resistive. The nontalker may simply feel a sense of hopelessness about the relationship. A person may be tired of trying and has simply given up. This type of nontalker may have been repeatedly hurt in this relationship or in similar relationships.

The silent one may be experiencing long-term burnout totally unrelated to the person or the group with whom he or she is not talking. Such a person might not have any additional energy to give to this relationship.

Sometimes the nontalker who knows what to say but doesn't say it, is being dragged into a conversation at the wrong time of the day, or finds the level of the conversation is too deep or too shallow to meet the nontalker's need.

3. They use nontalking as manipulation. Sometimes the nontalker has a sense of personal importance by smugly thinking, "You need me and my ideas, but I won't talk until you give me x, y, or z."

This nontalker is working a power play by refusing to talk. Frequently the power play gets results as the other person gives in. The end result, however, generally does not strengthen the relationship. Once manipulation starts, people tend to continue relating by manipulation rather than understanding.

Why People Should Want to Talk

A willingness to talk says something about you as a person and your values in life. Talking shows that you want some of the following things to take place.

Desire to be known. Appropriate talking indicates that you have enough confidence in yourself to share your ideas and feelings. It further indicates that you also have confidence in the person with whom you are talking. You believe that sharing your ideas and feelings will help your friend know you better, and you are willing to trust that person with this insight about you.

Desire to contribute, create, and help. Suppose you are in a group of five, a committee appointed to make suggestions to improve the missionary outreach of your church. If someone in the group does not talk, the rest of the group will think that person is uninterested. The group will silently conclude the person has no desire to contribute to the group's purpose.

As each person shares ideas, however, a sense of camaraderie grows. People are drawn together not only by the task, but by each person's willingness to get involved in the task by sharing insights.

Desire for friendship, fellowship, sharing. Talking is an extension of yourself to another person in a form that can be assimilated. As we eat, our body adds various enzymes and juices along the digestive tract to break down that food into a form that can be assimilated by our bodies. Talking is like a digestive process. We take the raw material of our inner self and digest it so that a new form—"words"—can then be presented to our friend.

Your friend knows you value him or her enough to go through that process.

Desire to accept responsibility. Most people react negatively when they are forced to read another person's mind. When someone says, "Do you think I'm a mind reader?" he is pleading for help and wanting the other person to talk. When you talk, you are not asking the other person to do your work for you, but you are accepting your responsibility in this relationship.

Desire to know the other person. When a person talks, revealing himself or herself by sharing ideas and feelings, an unspoken understanding prevails that this person wants the other to share information in return. One of the most affirming acts you can perform is to express to another person that you want to know him or her. As you talk about yourself and then allow the conversation to switch so that you are listening, you are expressing how deeply you value that person as a human being.

Preparing to Talk

All you have learned from this book about yourself and building friendships is background for developing your talking skills. To further prepare you to talk, we'll look at several more areas on the following pages.

Sensitivity. To be an effective talker you need to be sensitive to people. Think for a moment about some of the people you know who totally dominate a conversation. I could list a dozen men and women who absolutely run over me with words when we are together. If they aren't talking, they feel nothing significant is going on. It may be they feel so inadequate that they must keep filling the air with words. Or they may feel their insights are so important they must tell everything they know every time.

Insensitive talkers are not appreciated by other people. As you share, think of the needs of your friend. Focus your ideas toward her interests and needs.

Physical Setting. Physical factors also influence the effectiveness of your talking. Trying to carry on a deep and meaningful conversation while you are watching television, waiting in an elevator with other people, standing in the K-Mart checkout line, or playing tennis will not work too well. For meaningful talk, choose a quiet place without distractions.

Your physical appearance is also important. I'm not pushing you to buy a new wardrobe, but work with what you've got. Studies show that people who have a positive, clean appearance are more highly valued by others.

Let me put it to you bluntly: Look nice and smell nice. Brush your teeth. Use deodorant. Don't wear scuzzy clothes. Think of the other person. Try to match your appearance somewhat with your friend's, so that you aren't dressed too far up or down.

Peers. Conversation means that you are equals; you are peers. David Augsburger, in his book *Caring Enough to Hear and Be Heard,* talks about the importance of being equal in the communication. He suggests that there should be an equality of hearing each other and an equality of owning the conversation. Both people should be equally committed to the relationship.[2]

You should each bear an equal responsibility for the other and for keeping the relationship going. Both of you are accountable. In practical terms, don't lean on your friend to carry all the load of talking or listening.

Conflict. Before you start to talk, ask yourself what you're going to do when conflict arises. Recent studies show that we humans are "incredibly sensitive to criticism. Most people aren't eager to talk about the negative aspects of their relationships. They think it's unkind, or they find it embarrassing."[3]

Strangely, however, most people tend to ignore the good things that are happening in their relationships and only focus on a few negatives. Ask the question, "What will I do when we experience conflict?"

Quite often, when conflict arises, people become defensive. Think for a moment, "How can I diffuse defensiveness in this relationship?" These suggestions might help:

- Try to understand the other person's point of view.
- Feel with your friend. See through the eyes of that person's understanding.
- Try to make a clear statement that will incorporate your feelings and the feelings of your friend.
- Use "I" statements in place of "you" statements. "I" statements eliminate laying blame on the other person. It's less threatening when you say, "I feel lonely. I feel uneasy," than if you say, "You never pay any attention to me," or "What have you been doing? You're late again!"

Conflict will come, but conflict is a way for both of you to grow by broadening your point of view and understand each other.

Be interested in life. The more you know about what's happening in the world and especially in the lives of people, the more interesting you are. If you are a caring person who is aware of current events and you understand the stress felt by the people involved in those events, you will have something to talk about. As you communicate care for other people, your friend can understand that you also care for him or her.

How to Talk

I'm teasing, of course, when I tell you always be sure to talk with your mouth and tongue. Seriously, though, let's think about the mechanics of talking.

First, people who talk enthusiastically, with a sense of excitement about life, tend to be listened to more than people who talk in a slow, quiet, boring voice without any vocal animation.

Second, the tone of your voice may communicate more to the person who is listening than the words you use. A common complaint from wives is that their husbands don't tell them frequently enough that they love them. After the husband has been repeatedly nagged, he finally says, in a disgusted, grouchy voice, "Okay, I love you." He said the right words, but his tone of voice destroyed the meaning of the words. The tone of your voice should communicate warmth, caring, and sincerity.

Third, your nonverbals are an important aspect to consider as you think about how to talk. Are your facial expressions, body position, hands, and overall physical bearing consistent with the words you use? Now is the time to apply all of those attending skills you have been practicing since chapter 7. Those skills will help you to be a better talker so that your nonverbal body language is in line with your words.

One caution: Don't lose sight of your relationship as we focus on mechanics. Talking the right way can help, but true caring and interest will carry you a long way, even with imperfect talking skills. Mechanics are important, but I want you to move beyond the mechanics of talking to the life that exists between the two of you.

Hugh Prather, author of *Notes to Myself,* reminds us of the true heart of communication: "For communication to have meaning it must have a life. It must transcend 'you and me' and become 'us.' If I truly communicate, I see in you a life that is not me and partake of it. And you see and partake of me. In a small way we then grow out of our old selves and become something new. To have this kind of sharing I cannot enter conversation clutching myself. I must enter it with loose boundaries. I must give myself to the relationship, and be willing to be what grows out of it."[4]

What to Say

Start with your similarities. What are the common grounds between you? What are your similar interests, activities, values, and life concerns? These are what you should talk about. Your listening and attending skills should give you information about your friend so that you have a wealth of subjects to discuss.

Share your feelings. You might feel rather selfish sharing your feelings with your friend. But it is important for your friend's benefit that you share who you are, what you value, and your overall feelings about life.

The more you talk about your feelings and share yourself with others, the happier and more meaningful your life will be. Sometimes feelings are hard to share because you don't have adequate words. That's one of the limitations of our language. "Sanskrit (an old Eastern language) is reputed to have over 900 words describing various feeling states, but English has fewer than 50."[5]

It's natural to have emotions. They are an important indicator of what's going on inside of you. It's not physically healthy for you to suppress your feelings. If you do suppress them, both you and your friend will miss out on understanding the "real you."

Feelings are the internal, psychological, and physiological reactions to your experiences. As you experience life, your body may tremble or sweat, tears might come, or your heart might beat faster. You may experience several emotions at the same time, such as exhilaration, joy, sadness, or loneliness. Expressing your feelings opens up a window for your friend to peek inside and get to know you better.

Sometimes it's difficult to control your emotions. You may find yourself crying or laughing when you don't want to, or you may, on some occasions, feel that you are expressing your feelings inappropriately.

Remember: it's better to express emotions slightly inappropriately than not to express emotions at all. I hope you'll be able to be sensitive to your own feelings and the level of your friendship, and then choose which ones to express in which situations. But do express your feelings!

Risk your feelings. Trust and risk are intertwined. The more you trust a friend, the more you will be able to risk sharing your real self and feelings with that person. Remembering some of the following cautions about sharing and risk may help.

Risk and sharing should be appropriate. It would be inappropriate for a man to walk up to a woman who is a total stranger and say, "I love you. I want to kiss you." But that might be suitable in a growing relationship.

It would be inappropriate in a new relationship to talk about your childhood anxieties or even more inappropriate to share your fears that you are homosexual. But in a seasoned relationship those fears could be shared.

I'm encouraging you to share, but I don't mean that you emotionally take off your clothes and dance around the room naked. Your sharing must be appropriate to the person, the time, and the depth of the relationship.

Sharing should be gradual. Don't risk by sharing everything in the first heart-to-heart talk with a friend. Both of you should slowly reveal a little bit more about your life, values, and feelings. This process should go on during many different contacts, so that over a period of months you will gradually share your real selves with each other.

Sharing and risk-taking should be equal for both of you. You shouldn't do all of the risk-taking, thus getting yourself out on a limb, if your friend has not shared at all. Neither should you allow your friend to take all of the risk by sharing more deeply than you. It will be easier for both of you to keep confidences if you have risked equally.

Do you remember the story I told you in chapter 6 about the three preachers who revealed their secret sins to each other? The first two men were in extremely vulnerable positions because they had shared more rapidly and deeply than the third man. If they had known more about the third—that his secret sin was gossip—they would probably not have shared at all! Sharing must be equal, gradual, and appropriate.

The benefit of sharing is that "when a person has been able to disclose himself utterly to another person, he learns how to increase his contact with his real self, and he may then be better able to direct his destiny on the basis of knowledge of his real self."[6]

Talking is an important skill that will help you to develop as a person, as well as help your relationships to become more satisfying. As we come to the end of this chapter, I want you to choose a talking exercise to practice. Remember, this is not a book about ideas. It's a book through which you incorporate ideas into the routine of your life.

Individual Growth Activities

1. Sit in front of a mirror and talk to yourself. Express as accurately as possible your feelings and ideas. Then respond to yourself as if you are in a conversation. This practice should help you to express yourself as well as help you to get more in touch with your feelings. (Note: Do this when you are alone. If you do this in a public restroom, you may get locked up.)

2. Choose a friend with whom you have a degree of friendship established. When that friend seems to be ready to listen, share some of your feelings about your work, marriage, goals for life, or whatever. Risk a small amount and notice if you are encouraged to share more. Perhaps your talking will help your friend also to share more. Remember, as people talk and listen in risk areas, they tend to be bonded together.

Group Growth Activities

1. Each person should write five completions to the following phrase: "I am ..." The completed sentences might share a joy,

fear, aspiration, goal, frustration, and so on. After the statements are written, they should be shared and followed up with an explanation of the feelings behind the statements.

2. Form into groups of three, with one person talking and sharing, one listening, and the third evaluating the people doing the talking and listening. The evaluator should make positive comments about the strengths of the talking but should also report when "risk" was not taken or when only ideas and events were shared.

3. Since you have been meeting for some time, I suggest that as a group you decide what talking project you will each carry out during the week. At your next session, share what happened.

Chapter 10

Skill #4

Empathy: Caring Enough to Send Your Very Best

Now and then I come across stories that make me wonder about the human race. Two stories from an Orange County, California, newspaper on the same day show the problems we humans have in caring for one another.

TWO MEN ATTACK TIED LINEMAN
LEAVE HIM HANGING FROM LINE

.The lineman, stranded when the controls of his cherry picker bucket failed, was left dangling when his safety line froze. . . . Two men driving by stopped and asked the lineman how much he would pay them to help him. . . .

When the men learned to operate the cherry-picker, they ran it up and down with the lineman dangling from it. . . . With the worker hanging about a foot off the ground, the two men beat him unconscious. When he awoke, most of his clothes had been ripped off.[1]

128

In the same newspaper on the same day is another article entitled:

Warmth is denied element for shunned bag ladies

They are so different from us, all the shopping-bag ladies, because they have no homes.

They huddle in doorways and alleys, apparently unable to band together even for warmth, unable to provide for themselves in a society that doesn't see them. . . .

I met another homeless woman once, in front of my apartment door. She was just standing there, middle-aged, foreign, neat and clean as anyone else. . . .

At her feet were supermarket bags mysteriously laden with what seemed to be mounds of orange peels, Kleenex and paper towels tossed together in a disconcerting heap.

I entered my own apartment apprehensively, waiting for her to do something to justify my nervousness.

She knocked on the door within minutes. I knew that she wanted something, something strange.

"Can I use the bathroom?" she asked shyly.

"Of course," I said and led her there. She closed the door and I sat in the living room thinking the worst. . . .

After an hour, she emerged on tiptoe. I hoped she would disappear. She walked out the door without a word.

Hours later, on my way to dinner, I saw her. . . . She reached into a bag and drew out a Kleenex, then sidled up to me and blocked my way to the elevator.

She unraveled the Kleenex, revealing a twenty-dollar bill. "If I give you this, can I stay in your house?"

"I don't have room for you."

"No one does," she said.[2]

You Must Learn to Care

Being concerned for people, understanding them, seeing life through their eyes, and feeling with them are expressions of care or concern that I will refer to as "empathy." I want you to develop this caring skill, but don't think it's a brand-new one. You were born with it.

Even before birth, the fetus in the womb is aware of the world outside and the feelings of the mother. After birth, babies are sensitive to joy or pain. It's not something they have to learn; it's just there.

In fact, we learn **not** to care for people. As we go through life, we realize that it's not necessary to be caring for everyone. As a result, we grow more sensitive to important people such as our bosses or people who have positions that can help or harm us, but we also learn to cut out people who are unimportant or whom we view as inferior.

The encouraging fact is that at whatever level our empathy skills might be now, they can be improved. In one study, twenty-eight older adults were randomly assigned to three different groups. One group, the "training group," received special training in empathy; another group just discussed the problems of people; and a third group did nothing but take an evaluation test.

"For eight weeks the training group practiced empathy as a helping skill. . . . Unlike the [other] groups, the training group improved significantly on three measures of empathy. The training group also showed significant gains in self-exploration."[3]

Don't be discouraged if you think you have a low level of caring for people. You can learn! If you knew everything about relationships, you wouldn't be reading this book, and we never would have started this written conversation. So let's launch into learning the skill of empathy.

What Is Empathy?

A study was conducted at Princeton Seminary to test the empathy level of students preparing for ministry. Each student was asked to deliver a brief talk on the Good Samaritan story from the Bible. The students were then told to go to the recording studio to record their talk.

> While in transit, each passed a victim slumped in the alley, head down, eyes closed, coughing and groaning.
> Some of the students had been sent off knowing they had plenty of time: 'It will be a few minutes before they're ready for you. If you have to wait over there, it shouldn't be long.' Of these, most stopped to offer aid. Others, however, had been told, 'You're late. They were expecting you a few minutes ago so you'd better hurry.' Of these, only 10 percent offered help. Conclusion? Hurried people are likely to pass by people in distress, even if they are hurrying to speak on the parable of the Good Samaritan.[4]

The word **empathy** comes from two Greek words. One word, from which we get our word **pathos,** means "to feel deeply"; the other is a prefix which means "in" or "into." So empathy means "to feel deeply into another person's life."

I suggest you think of empathy as looking through someone else's eyeballs. Imagine getting inside that person's head and skin to see, feel, and understand life as he or she does.

When you are empathetic, you deliberately identify with your friend's feelings. You are empathetic when you see life from another's point of view. You need to get far enough into your friend's feelings to truly understand and experience his or her feelings and to suffer or rejoice with that person.

When you begin to feel compassion and empathy for another person, changes take place in your body. Blood pressure, heart rate, perspiration, and overall physical tenseness increase. In a sense, your body is reaching out to the other person.

Empathy is "being with someone." Jesus is a classic model of empathy for us. The Scripture calls him "Emmanuel," that is, "God with us." The picture of Jesus in the Gospels is that of a person of compassion who understands the human situation and meets people at the point of their need.

Jesus was filled with compassion as he healed the leper. When the widow of Nain lost her son, he was moved with compassion. He looked over the city of Jerusalem and felt compassion, recognizing their tremendous need, which, tragically, they were unwilling to acknowledge.

Raising Lazarus from the dead, healing the blind man who asked for sight, these incidents and dozens of others show Jesus as a man of compassion. If you start reading a chapter a day from the gospel of John, you will see how caring and empathetic Jesus was to people then—and to you now.

Jesus' care is not past tense. The Scripture says, "Jesus the Son of God is our great high priest who has gone to heaven itself to help us. . . . This High Priest of ours understands our weaknesses, since he had the same temptations we do. . . . so let us come boldly to the very throne of God and stay there to receive his mercy and to find grace to help us in our times of need."[5]

Jesus' compassion is available for us **now**. As we experience his deep caring for us, we learn how to express caring to a friend. This deep caring—empathy—helps relationships grow.

Ways to Express Empathy

1. Our **bodies** involuntarily express empathy. As you share something with a close and empathetic friend, you'll notice your friend's face and body communicate understanding and iden- tification with your feelings. Your friend may frown, smile, laugh, or cry. Your friend's body visibly lets you know he or she is tuned in.

When you listen empathetically to a friend, you too will passionately understand and feel with your friend. Allow your body to respond so your friend knows you care. Relax for a moment and deliberately stop worrying about how you are impressing your friend. Give your eyes, facial muscles, hands, and general body tension free reign to communicate, "I'm with you in this happy time in your life," or "I understand the deep agony that you're going through."

2. The **tone** of your voice can also communicate empathy. People pick up from your voice whether you're harsh or sensitive to their feelings. If this is a sad time, talk quieter and at a slower pace. If the occasion is happy, speak louder at a faster pace with a smile in your words.

3. **Words** are a tool. You need to say directly, "I love you," "I'm with you," "I care about the hurt you're experiencing," or "I'm so very happy for this great success in your life."

4. **Touching** is another way to communicate empathy. Again, Jesus becomes an example for us. He frequently touched people. He could have only spoken the word of healing to the leprous man; instead Jesus reached out and touched him.[6] For the blind man he made a mudpack and put it on his eyes, touching him.[7] Again, he touched Jairus's daughter when he brought her back to life.[8] He touched the tongue of the deaf and dumb man.[9] It was common for Jesus to reach out and touch people or to let them touch him.

Frequently, as a pastor, I've been with people who are in great pain or who have experienced profound loss. What do you say to a mother and father whose son has just been accidentally electrocuted? What words can help parents whose baby has died from sudden crib death? What can you say to a woman whose husband has just told her he has never loved her and is filing for a divorce?

Many times in human experience words are totally inadequate. Last night while visiting a friend in the hospital, I just reached down and patted her hand. My friend was in great pain following surgery, so we just quietly held hands with tears in our eyes.

Think of today. Were there appropriate ways you could have touched people, to let them know that you care for them? Each day look for some way to touch another person. Consider holding a handshake a little longer or pat someone on the back or maybe give a good hug.

5. Your physical **presence** also communicates empathy. You don't need to say anything. Sometimes talking raises the anxiety level of the person. But your presence creates an invisible bond that says, "You're important to me."

6. Giving a person your **time** also communicates empathy. I'm repeatedly amazed as I look at the frequently interrupted schedule of Jesus' life. But the purpose of Jesus' presence on earth was not to travel, give speeches, or confront the religious leaders. He was on earth to minister to people. Anytime a person wanted his attention, he or she got it. His life seems so unplanned to me, yet Christ was totally in control. His schedule actually was never interrupted. People **were** his program!

My problem is that I have to write books and articles. I have conferences to lead, radio and television appearances to make, classes to teach, and employees to oversee. As a result, some people who want my help seem like an intrusion on my precious schedule.

I confess to you that it's not very empathetic of me to care more about my schedule than about people. Oh, I know. I can justify it. I can say, "Hey look, I'm helping thousands more people by rushing off to do all of these things, rather than giving attention to this one person." Yet somehow I still see Jesus repeatedly turning his attention away from the large groups and focusing on one individual.

When you give a person some of your time, you are giving a portion of your life. Because of the gift of your time, people sense that you genuinely care for them.

What Limits or Distorts Empathy?

Individualism. We think "individual" instead of "group." We think "I" instead of "we." We emphasize how different we are rather than how similar we are. We say we have come from a unique community. We talk of the cute things in our apartment or our home. We speak of our individual creativity at work or leisure. Our individualism is seen in our home decorations, cooking, sports, hobbies, and in our stories and humor.

Perhaps the problem is that we live in such an impersonal society that we're forced to establish our individual identities. Many times we become so individualistic that it is almost impossible to deeply understand another human being.

Empathy comes easier when our friend has many similarities that we understand. If, however, we repeatedly put ourselves in an absolutely unique category, then it will be difficult to relate to any other human being. Yes, we should be individuals, but we also need to look for the many areas of life we have in common.

Infallibility. "Nothing gets in the way of empathy more than the bland assumption of infallibility. . . . Uncomfortable as it may be, belief in one's own fallibility makes the development of empathy with others much easier."[10] When you think you are perfect, you become the standard of the universe and everyone else misses the mark. Everyone else becomes inferior to you.

There is an arrogance in feeling perfect. That arrogance will blind you from understanding other people. Self-declared perfect people tend to say to themselves, "Well, I did it. Why can't they? If they'd try a little harder, they could make it like I did."

If, on the other hand, you recognize that you are a vulnerable human being, you will be more empathetic toward others. Remember, the circumstances of your life could change at any moment. Suddenly, **you** could be confronted by a sudden illness, loss of a limb, rape, bankruptcy, stroke, heart attack, betrayal by your closest friend, and on and on.

We are frail human beings, living, as it were, by fine threads in a spider's web. When our friends are hit by sudden misfortune, we should offer them care—not our perfection.

Let me ask, would you like me better if I told you how great I am? Or do you like me better if I talk freely about the fact that I blow it in my relationships with God, my wife, and other people?

I'm an ordinary human being who has experienced some successes and a number of colossal failures. I would encourage you not to let your successes, seeming perfection, and infallibility cause you to be aloof so that you are unable to be empathetic.

People as objects. Empathy can play tricks on your mind. Maybe it's just that **my** mind plays tricks on **me.** Sometimes, when I'm being empathetic toward people, before I know what's happening, I start to congratulate myself about how warm, caring, understanding, and tender I am.

This deception may subtly lead us to keep these people in a needy position. We like them to be needy so that we can continue to crank out empathy and feel good about ourselves.

When we need our friends to need us, we have dehumanized them into objects or "needy projects" that make us feel good. Now the energy is not flowing from us toward them to enrich their lives; the energy is bouncing back to us. That type of empathy is self-serving.

When your empathy starts to refocus on you, it has become a tool for manipulation. You may continue to offer help to people who don't need help, because you have a need to get their returned affirmation. Ask yourself, "Is my empathy focusing on caring for my friends, or am I meeting my own needs?"

How to Increase or Expand Your Empathetic Skill

Remember, as a baby you were born with the marvelous capacity to be empathetic toward other people. Have you ever noticed what happens when several babies are put together and one of them starts to cry? Frequently, the others also begin to cry. There's spontaneous empathy as children identify with the one who is crying.

Since birth you may have learned to selectively shut down your empathy. I encourage you to open up those empathetic valves. Let those good juices flow again. You will then better understand and care for your friends.

Perhaps we're back to the main question: **How do you develop, establish, and maintain friendships? Answer: you serve people at the point of their need.**

Being empathetic, then, is a crucial skill for serving people. Let's look at some of the ways that you can increase or enlarge your empathetic gift.

Skills build skills. By now you realize that I've been pushing you to reevaluate some of your personal philosophies toward people. I've also been urging you to practice different skills and new attitudes. I want you to become a freed-up person who really loves people.

The meaning of the Barbra Streisand song is very accurate: "People who need people are the luckiest people in the world." God made you to be a lover of people. My goal is to help that gift become a reality in your daily life.

All of the skills you are learning are intertwined. Each one influences the others. When you ask, "How can I enlarge my empathetic skills?" the answer is that you need to practice **attending, listening,** and **talking.** You must also have an increasingly positive view of yourself. Keep on expanding all those qualities and attitudes, such as being nonjudgmental, accepting, and trusting, which we talked about in chapter 6.

Without realizing it, as you practice the other skills, you are also building your empathetic skills. That's the fun part about growing to become a better friend. Each skill helps the other skills to develop and friendships are the result.

We are more empathetic if we think other people are similar to us. Think about that point for a moment. The authors of *The Human Connection* report, "In ... empathy studies, observers responded more empathetically if they were led to believe the victim was similar to themselves. The perception of similarity seems to heighten the subjects' sensitivity to the reaction of the other person and to make it easier for them to imagine they were in his or her place.... The perception of differences creates barriers."[11]

The more you understand other people, the more you realize how similar you are to them and the easier it is for you to be empathetic. Think of yourself as being in your friend's shoes. Identify the things you hold in common with your friend. Focusing on your common backgrounds or experiences will encourage your empathy. This idea of similarity flows into the next point.

Expose yourself to different people. In the pastoral counseling class I taught for students preparing for ministry, I asked them to practice their listening skills with people who were different from themselves. They were required to listen to a dying person, a mid-life person, a person of the opposite sex, a total stranger, a teenager, and their mate.

The students repeatedly evaluated these listening experiences as significant for their growth because it pushed them into contacts with people who were different. Students were stretched to grasp new perspectives on life, they became less rigid, they didn't have as many quick answers for life, and their capacity for empathy took a big leap forward.

So here we go again. Here's another one of those little projects I want you to work on. Ask yourself, "How can I expose myself to other people?" Let me suggest some people or groups with whom you can develop your empathy skills:

- talk to a bag lady
- listen to a mid-life woman
- talk to a rich man

- talk to a retired couple; ask them what it feels like to be "unemployed"
- visit a convalescent home
- invite a minority family to your home for dinner
- invite a missionary to stay at your house
- ride for an evening in a police car, listening as the officers interact with life
- visit a jail and talk to inmates
- you are creative—generate some of your own ideas

I've traveled widely around the world. Each time I confront a new culture, I grow. I become more understanding and empathetic. But some of my biggest empathetic improvements have come through intensive listening to people who live nearby.

Joe, a close friend, taught me a lot about life. He is now in the presence of the Lord. Joe served in a number of different positions in our church from Sunday-school teacher and chairman of the board of deacons to chairman of the board of leadership. He was a tremendously godly man who had his head screwed on right and loved people. Joe helped me learn to love more broadly and to become more empathetic.

Oh, I forgot to tell you a few things about Joe—traits about him that should have kept a good, upright WASP like me from learning from him. Joe was black. On top of that, he enjoyed being black. He felt that the black culture had a lot to contribute to America.

Another thing I forgot to tell you about Joe is that he was stricken with polio during World War II and was paralyzed from the chest down. He was confined to a wheelchair. Most of us are afraid of disabled people. We try to smile and be polite, but we often treat them as freaks.

Joe couldn't move his legs and had to be lifted in and out of his wheelchair. He also had to have a special bed at home that would help him breathe. His wife had to use a respirator on him frequently. She also had to use a suction machine to vacuum mucus out of his throat because he didn't have muscle strength to clear his throat or to cough.

Boy, doesn't that turn you off? We like perfection, Mr. Universe, Miss America. We like everything put together just right, looking great, none of this imperfection junk.

But Joe was terrific. He was warm, intelligent, sensitive, caring, and a spiritual man who also loved me. I cry as I think about his acceptance and love of me. He loved me in spite of my intolerance, immaturity, and lack of developed empathy. Wow, what a terrific guy!

I forgot to tell you one other thing. You see, I had been taught that charismatic people were bad. Speaking in tongues meant that the person was at the least misguided, maybe even emotionally deranged. They might be tools of Satan actually preaching a satanic message.

One time Joe let the deacons and me know he spoke in tongues. During a deacons' meeting, he quietly said, "You know, brothers, when I pray to God, I speak in a heavenly language. It isn't something I sought; it just happened. One time I was so in awe of God, I simply started to speak in tongues."

Well, I sat there dumbfounded. How can this be happening right here in my deacons' meeting? How can this wonderful guy who has taught me so much be saying that he speaks in tongues?

But God was continuing to do good things in me as he allowed me to see that God isn't a Baptist nor a Presbyterian, Catholic, Episcopalian, or Pentecostal. God is God! Our expressions of worship, tragically, have sometimes become the basis to divide us rather than draw us together.

It isn't just Baptists or charismatics who are saved. Anybody—from whatever church background or with no background at all—anybody who places faith in Jesus Christ is a believer.

So let your world expand! Be brave! Talk to other people! Develop friendships with Christians who worship differently than you do. Why not even become a friend with an agnostic? Exposure to new people will be frightening at first, but it will be exciting as you watch your empathy grow.

Observe people. Everything people do has a conscious or unconscious choice behind it. As you carefully observe people, it will help you to understand them. Look at their body language as well as their lifestyle. Do they wear glasses or contacts? Observe their makeup, fingernails, clothes, shoes, wristwatch, wallet or purse, car, office, home, yard, furniture, dishes, stereo, books, hobbies—the list is endless. Everything about people gives you a clue as to who they are. All of these clues can become the basis for building sensitivity or empathy into your life.

After you have carefully observed someone, then put yourself in that person's shoes and ask how it would feel to be that person. What would I think? How would I respond to life?

As a boy growing up in Cleveland, Ohio, I frequently rode city buses. Riding a bus is basically boring. So to occupy my time I looked at the people seated around me. I tried to imagine what they did, where they came from, what they were thinking, what they liked or didn't like. At the time I didn't realize it, but I was developing sensitivity.

I still watch people. In fact, I frequently refer to myself as a professional people watcher. I like to watch people, and I still ask some of the same questions I asked when I was young.

Go ahead. Observe people. I'm not asking you to be a nut by staring at people or to become a peeping Tom. But watching people will help you grow in empathy.

Use your own experience. By now, you've lived a few years. You've experienced some fun times and some bad times. When somebody else has struggles, you should be able to draw from your reservoir of experience to understand that person. How did it feel when you experienced hardship, isolation, or tragedy? What was going on inside you when you were angry, hostile, or felt closed off from people? How did you feel when you had success or felt loved and appreciated or won an honor?

As you re-feel your own feelings in similar situations, it will help you to be empathetic with your friend. Now be careful. When your friend starts to tell you about what he or she is feeling, don't jump in and say, "Oh, yeah, yeah, I had that feeling. Let me tell you about my experience." Remember to use your listening skills. Let your friend talk. Your face and your "uh-huhs" can carry a clear, unspoken understanding, "I know what you're experiencing. I've been there, I've felt those things, I'm feeling it all again with you. I care about you."

Imagination. Obviously, you can't experience everything in life or even everything your friend is going through. But you can develop your imagination to assist you to get a grip on what your friend is experiencing.

By now you realize that I am male. You also may have gathered that Sally and I have three daughters. Obviously, I don't know what it's like to be pregnant. I know a little bit about what it's like to be sick and vomit. I hate to vomit. I would rather be sick two extra days than to vomit once. Sally was always very sick for the first four or five months of each pregnancy. Since I understand a little about vomiting because of personal experience, I understand a little bit about pregnancy.

But I don't understand what it feels like to have your breasts enlarge, your abdomen start to get full, feel the first movement of the child inside your body, and then the increasingly vigorous kicking, moving, and squirming of a child inside you. I don't know any of those feelings from experience. But I do understand more about pregnancy as I listen to Sally talk and as I let my imagination work. There were times when I could come close to feeling with her what was going on.

I also don't know anything about childbirth from personal experience. To be honest, I don't want to know. I can't imagine, even though I've tried to, how those bones spread so widely apart. That's such a small opening, and yet that large baby's head comes down the birth canal and out through those pelvic bones. Think of those broad shoulders passing through. Wow, the pain, the stress! But then the exhilaration of birth. A child, a life that has grown in you. You're holding your own child in your hands.

What does it feel like to hold your own flesh and blood against your breast? Men never know the pleasantness of having their breast nuzzled by their own child. What is the joy a woman realizes as she nurses a life that is a combination of her life and of her husband who deeply loves her?

No, I've never felt any of those things physically, but I have felt those things through my mind as I've talked to Sally, allowing my imagination to run free.

Let your imagination carry you into some new depths of empathy and understanding. For the next few days, for instance, practice imagining what people are thinking and why they make certain choices. Imagine what a person's greatest stress or greatest happiness in life might be. See if you can pick up a few small clues. Then let your imagination carry you into some new territory.

Remember, what you imagine is not necessarily the truth, but it is a helpful practice that will develop your sensitivity. Then when a friend does share feelings, you will be better able to empathize.

Deep relationships. "Research evidence shows that people who have not been loved are incapable of loving," say some experts.[12] This is a dog-chasing-the-tail problem. If you've not been deeply loved by other people and experienced their empathy, then you probably are going to have trouble empathizing with and loving other people. Once you experience love from other people, it is easier for you to empathize. Once you have been deeply understood, it's easier for you to understand others.

You may ask, "How do I get into the circle of empathetic love?" You can jump into the circle at any point. In fact, you **must** get into this circle if you are going to experience growth in your life. One way of jumping in is by using some of your other skills. Listen and attend to people as Christ would. As you begin to use your skills, caring relationships will grow. You will then receive nurturance, empathy, understanding, love, and care from other people. As you receive more of those positive expressions, it will be easier for you to be empathetic in return.

Remember, you **must** jump into the circle and get the process started. In some ways it's easy to do because you were born with some of these skills. They might have been stifled, but you've already been practicing the friendship skills that are going to help you rekindle your empathy.

The deeper your relationships, the more you will understand people. The more you understand people, the greater is the potential for your empathy skills to develop.

Practice your skills. As this chapter closes, I am suggesting some skill-development activities that you can do individually or with a small group. Please remember, this is not just a book of ideas. If you don't practice, you probably won't change. So hang tough. Be brave. Start pushing out in some of these practice areas.

As you live out an empathetic lifestyle, you will become more human and alive. Your friends also will have more hope in life, knowing that you genuinely understand and love them. That's powerful stuff for long-term relationships.

Individual Growth Activities

Develop your empathetic skill by doing an activity similar to the following:

- listen to a variety of people such as those suggested on pages 138–39
- take a bag of groceries to a poor family
- imagine how each person feels who is shown on the evening news
- sit in a shopping mall and imagine the greatest sadness or joy of specific people who pass by

Group Growth Activities

Be creative—this week you're on your own to design activities that will increase your capacity to be empathetic.

Chapter 11

Skill #5

Genuineness: Being Real in a Phony World

Rich, a college friend of mine, seemed to do everything in life to win the approval of other people. His eyes had a rather pathetic, empty look that said, "Tell me, what can I do to make you like me?" Rich would modify his behavior, change his clothes, or express an opinion exactly the opposite of what he had said a few minutes earlier to make you like him. He was willing to do whatever you wanted, go where you wanted, think as you wanted him to think. The problem was that you never really knew Rich.

Rich was not a Christian, but because we attended a Christian college, he played the role of a Christian. He used Christian language, attended church, read Christian books so that he could discuss them, even joined a local church. In essence, Rich was not a person; he was an accumulation of strings that other people pulled.

Some people try so hard to win your friendship that you don't know who they actually are. The actor Peter Sellers was interviewed by *Time* magazine just before he died. *Time* quoted one of his friends as saying, "Peter is the accumulation of all the roles he's played and all the people he's met." One time when Peter Sellers appeared with the Muppets, Kermit the Frog encouraged him to "relax and be yourself." Sellers reply is a tragic revelation of a nonperson. He said, "I could never be myself. You see, there is no me. I do not exist."[1]

My college friend and Peter Sellers are examples of people who are not real, who always play to an audience, always try to win someone's affection. In the process, sadly, they become nonpersons.

A further tragedy is that the unreal person desperately tries to win the approval of others. But people inherently reject those in whom they see no identity.

If I know who you really are, then I can choose to be or not to be your friend. But if I don't know who you are, then I have no basis for deciding whether I want to be your friend.

Another friendship skill you must learn, then, is to be a real person. True friendships cannot develop unless both people are willing to be genuine.

The Skill to Be Learned

Many words describe this skill of being real. **Congruence** is a technical term that means you are the same person with people as you are by yourself. You are the same with one group of people as with another. Congruence suggests openness, a transparency, a willingness to let other people know who you are. It assumes you have a pretty good understanding of yourself, that you are a person who is vulnerable and able to take risks by letting other people know you.

The skill we are learning is that of **appropriate self-disclosure that enables another person to know you as you really are.**

For you to learn this skill, I'm going to push you into risk-taking experiences. I'll ask you to be more vulnerable, transparent, and open than you've been before. I'm not going to ask you to bare your deepest secrets to strangers, but with gentle determination, I want you gradually to talk about who you really are with your friends.

Why Self-Disclosure Is Important

As you become more real, open, self-disclosing, transparent, and vulnerable, you will experience dramatic personal growth. Your realness will strongly affect the depth and quality of your friendships. Furthermore, your openness will cause personal growth in the lives of your friends as they better understand you, themselves, and the world of people.

You grow. Dr. Paul Tournier said, "It is impossible to overemphasize the need humans have to be really listened to, to be taken seriously, to be understood.... No one can develop freely in this world and find a full life without feeling understood by at least one person.... He who would see himself clearly must open up to a confidante freely chosen and worthy of such trust."[2]

When I speak of being real, I mean your willingness to disclose yourself to another person. Being real includes being known by sharing your feelings, ideas, fears, doubts, and even your past experiences of failure and success. Sharing these, along with your hopes for the future, will build strong friendships.

Sharing will also be a positive influence on your growth. The more you are trapped in your private little world with your own thoughts, the more likely you are to be an incomplete human being.

As you share yourself with another, you take a risk, but that risk also becomes an open door to provide you with feedback, affirmation, and a test of reality. As you share, others are also likely to share.

Men become fully men. Males in our society seem to have more difficulty than women with being real, open, and self-disclosing. "Women are the undisputed intimacy specialists in our society."[3] Boys are trained to be tough. Girls are trained to care. Boys are trained to suck it all up, stuff their feelings deep down inside, not cry—to be a "big man." Girls are treated more tenderly and encouraged to share their feelings.

Women tend to develop friendships on the basis of their shared lives and feelings. Men tend to develop friendships because of common activities—fishing, golf, football, sailing, or business ventures.

I've known a number of men who have been partners in business and fishing or golfing buddies. These men think of themselves as close friends. Yet one of them is very surprised when the other suddenly divorces his wife and breaks off the friendship with his buddy. These men thought of themselves as friends, yet they never really knew each other or what was going on inside the other.

Until recently, our society has convinced men that it is not manly to share feelings or to talk about problems or life's questions. Men have been persuaded they are inferior, sissies, or perhaps even homosexual if they express their feelings or disclose their inner selves.

But as a man begins to talk about his feelings, he discovers a whole second side to his personality. A new depth of caring for people emerges. He may find himself moved by emotion, even to the point of experiencing "leaky eyes."

At first, he may be startled and try to suppress these changes. But if he encourages this new development, he will become a full man in the sense that Jesus was. Jesus was able to make the tough decisions and go through the incredible crucifixion experience, yet he wept over people's sins and talked to kids whom he invited to sit on his lap. He truly was totally a man.

It fits God's plan. At the beginning of creation God said, "It isn't good for man to be alone."[4] It is not emotionally healthy for you to be in isolation. Your personality will be healthier, more complete, and more able to interact with other people as you disclose yourself to close friends.

Almost everyone is afraid of self-disclosure at some time in their lives. Many people believe if they tell you about themselves, they will lose power. They are afraid of losing control in the relationship or of being exploited.

Exactly the opposite is true. It may appear at the moment that you lose power if you become more vulnerable to another person, but the opposite happens. You gain insight into yourself and into your friend, and you cause your relationship to deepen. The bond of commitment between the two of you is more strongly cemented.

Self-disclosure is scary, but it definitely will help you to grow as a person and cause your relationships to be deeper and more lasting.

Your friend will grow. As two people begin to relate to each other, each person is deciding what to share and what not to risk. If we refuse to share ourselves, the other person will not open up either. Result: We learn nothing about the other person.

Start by sharing the safe bits and pieces to learn a little about the other person. For example, suppose at a party someone says, "Hello, my name's John Lewis, and I just moved into the community from Connecticut." John has shared information with you about himself, and he has clearly indicated he would like to talk to you. Most people will respond by sharing the same level of information. "My name's Jane Thompson. I'm new here, also. I came from Iowa."

But if Jane doesn't respond at all, John will try a few other sentences and finally give up and go away. If Jane responds but continues to give answers only at the same level as their opening comments, John will still get discouraged. If, on the other hand, Jane responds warmly by using good attending and listening skills, she will be able to draw John out to talk about where he used to live, why he moved here, as well as some of his hopes and dreams for the future.

If she also gradually shares her feelings about moving, along with her hopes and fears for the future, John will feel freer to talk about himself, and the relationship will deepen.

Without either of them planning on it, they each grow and change because they shared—disclosed—themselves with the other. Besides the personal growth they experience, they also enjoy friendship, mutual support, understanding, security, trust, appreciation, and love.

The experience of being another person's friend makes both people in the relationship feel better about themselves. "Someone else really understands me. I've been able to share some of my inner self and I was not rejected. That person still likes me. Wow!" That's a terrific feeling.

Disclosing the hidden self causes peace. The two circles on the following page visually show the process that should take place as you disclose yourself to your friend. Notice in circle A that the major portion of the circle representing our real selves is selectively hidden from new friends.

At the beginning of a relationship we only reveal safe, selected areas. In addition, parts of our personalities that are not fully understood by ourselves are, obviously, not revealed to our new friend. As a result, at the beginning of a friendship, only a small percentage of our real self is revealed.

Circle B, however, shows what should happen as you gradually disclose yourself to your friend. Notice that the percentage representing the revealed self is now the largest percentage. The section that you deliberately hide from your friend is now a much smaller percentage. Also notice the percentage of yourself that you didn't understand is also reduced in size. Your friendship has helped you better understand yourself as well as your friend.

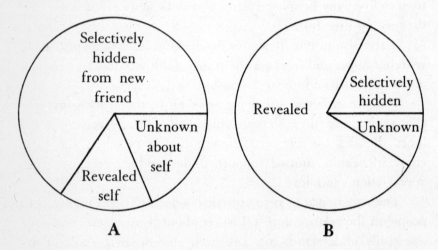

Self-revelation with a trusted, accepting friend creates a deep peace in you. If the hidden part of you is large, you will never really know if people like you as you really are or only for what you do for them.

In any friendship you will probably always keep a segment of yourself selectively hidden—a part of you that is known only to God. But it should be the goal in your friendships to make the two sections—the "selectively hidden" and the "unknown about yourself"—as small percentages as possible. As these areas decrease in size with trusted friends, your level of peace and self-esteem will increase.

One other comment about the importance of exercising the skill of self-disclosure: If you don't disclose yourself, you will frustrate yourself and your friend.

Suppose you are similar to my college friend, Rich, whom I

mentioned at the beginning of this chapter; that is, you always try to conform to what your friend wants you to feel, think, or be. If you give a false revelation of your real self, the other person can only respond to what he or she sees or hears. Your friend is likely to respond to your false information with a response that will not be satisfying to you, because that person is responding to a false you. When your friend responds to a false you, you will probably be hurt. When you are hurt, you will likely hurt back or withdraw from the friendship.

If you do not exercise the skill of honest self-disclosure, your relationships will be doomed because you both will be reacting to false information. Being open with your friend is not an option; it is the lifeblood of your relationship.

What Inhibits Openness

Many things could keep you from being open with your friends—your family background, your own incomplete development, or even an attitude or expression your friend uses that turns you off.

Generally, we are more willing to be open with people we like than with people we dislike. But each of us has our own quirks or inhibitors that keep us from being open. It would be helpful to identify those inhibitors in your life and work to reduce them.

Personally I find it difficult to be open with people whom I view as more powerful than I am. Since I am quite competitive, it is difficult for me to be open with people I view as "the competition." I also find it difficult to be open with women whom I view as extremely sexually attractive. In each of these cases, I feel I might lose control or power.

Think about your own life. What are your hang-ups? As I have worked to identify my fears, it has helped me to be more open in those fearful relationships.

Let's look at some of the common fears that restrict openness or self-disclosure. Maybe we'll touch on yours.

Fear of not being respected. If you have a higher position than your friend, such as in your career, you may fear that your friend will not respect your position and insights if you share your inner self. You may be afraid of looking weak to that person.

For example, usually a boss or a foreman will not share inner feelings for fear of losing a position of authority with you. They think, "People won't respect me if they see my weaknesses." This, by the way, is the trap of the average pastor. Sometimes marriage partners also feel devalued if they share a weakness.

Fear of losing a friend. "If I tell this person what I am really like, I might be rejected." You might think to yourself, "It's better to have part of a relationship than to risk it all by going for a deeper relationship."

Fear of being exploited. "If I tell my friend this secret, it might be used against me."

Dave, a friend of mine, is an associate pastor. He was asked to speak at a men's conference for another church. At the same time his unmarried college-age daughter revealed she was pregnant. Dave felt he wanted to share this concern with someone to receive the prayer support he and his family desperately needed.

He chose to share his burden with his local evangelical ministerial association whom he looked upon as brothers and confidantes. But one of the men from the group, a gossip, passed on the confidential information to the church that had invited Dave to speak at the conference. Within days, the church withdrew their invitation. Dave's family problem had been the basis of betrayal by the so-called friend.

Fear of being smothered. Sometimes a person doesn't want to share what's going on inside for fear of surrendering control to another person. That person doesn't want to be smothered or "mothered" by the caring friend who will try to take over the situation and straighten it out.

Fear of confrontation. A person may think, "If I share this with my friend, she may tell me to give up a habit, change a lifestyle, or stop a relationship. I'm not ready to do that yet." The person doesn't share for fear that the other person won't carefully listen or understand where she is in this process. She is afraid the friend will only offer confrontational advice, which will make the friend feel good but leave the one doing the sharing feeling isolated or put down.

Fear of the responsibility caused by self-knowledge. "If I open up this can of worms with my friend, then I'll have to face it, accept reality, take responsibility, and bear the shame or guilt associated with it," a person may rationalize. "I'm not yet ready to tackle this problem, so I'll continue to pretend it doesn't exist."

Fear of the reverse halo effect. The "halo effect" refers to the phenomenon that a person judged to be competent in one area is likely to be judged competent in other areas (even when that isn't true). For instance, if a person is an expert in psychology, an aura of expertise tends to spread to other areas. People may look upon this person's pronouncements in theology or political science with the same respect as his or her psychological insights.

The reverse "halo effect" sometimes stands in the way of self-disclosure. "If [a person] tells the other members about incompetence in one area of living, he feels that they will assume similar incompetence or irresponsibility in related or even unrelated areas."[5] Thus, a psychology expert probably would not share a personal weakness in money management for fear that people would then feel he or she was also incompetent in psychology.

As you can see, we may use many reasons to justify why we are hesitant to be open with our friend. But each of these reasons needs to be explored and tested to see if they are based on real or false fears.

A good way to test these fears is to use the "trial-balloon" method. Suppose that you have a fear of losing your friend if you tell her too much. Send up a trial balloon. Reveal a small part of your life and watch how your friend reacts. Does your friend pull away or draw closer as you allow her to know more about you? If your friend draws closer, test with a little more information. Continue this process until you discover how far you can trust her.

Not all people can be trusted equally. Many of the fears we have talked about are extremely legitimate with certain of your acquaintances. But don't assume that every one of your friends is totally untrustworthy. Test each friend to discover the ones with whom you can have deep and lasting friendships. I've learned that people vary greatly. Open up to each person only as much as that person can handle.

How to Develop the Skill of Self-Disclosure

Self-disclosure, like all of the other skills we have looked at, is something you can learn. As you've read through this chapter, you've already learned something about the important contribution self-disclosure can make to your life. The process is under way. Now let's turn our attention to concrete steps that will help this skill to become part of you.

Become tired of separateness. The first step toward any change is to recognize that we are uncomfortable where we are. When your feel a deep-seated desire for something different, something more, you have taken the first step toward developing a new skill. You have already expressed the desire for a change by picking up this book and reading this far.

John Denver sings a song entitled "Islands." He points out that people often live like islands in an ocean, separated from each other. The song sums up the sense of separateness and isolation, telling us that dreamers are always alone. As the song continues, John appeals for us to recognize that we are much more than just islands.

You are a separate person, but you need to relate to others. You were made for much more than isolation.

Have you ever wondered, "If I were sick and unable to move out of my bed for two days, would anybody know, care, or come looking for me?" Even more, what if someone called and said, "We noticed you were not at work, but someone else filled in for you"?

It would be bad enough not to be missed for two days, but how much more tragic it would be if you were only missed for what you could do—not because you had a friendship relationship with someone.

When you come to the point in your soul where you are deeply sick and tired of separateness and aloneness, you are ripe for risking more realness in relationships. When the fear of risk seems like only a small headache compared to the massive pain in your heart and stomach caused by the gnawing sense of loneliness, you have taken the first step toward preparation for self-disclosure.

Risk vulnerability in small steps. You've settled the issue. You've decided to risk self-disclosure so that your friendships will grow. You need to trust someone. You want to be in trusting relationships.

The second step is to realize that you don't need to disclose all of yourself to any one person, nor do you need to disclose yourself to everyone you meet.

The procedure of small steps of self-disclosure works like this. First identify the people with whom you would like to have deeper or longer relationships.

Try a small amount of self-disclosure gradually with one friend at a time. If you disclose too much too fast, that friend may become frightened and abandon you. If your self-disclosure is met by silence or shock you will likely not share with this person again.

When your friend is doing the sharing, it is important for you to speak assurances. Even your simple "uh-huh" will give assurance. But consider longer statements such as: "Thank you for sharing that," "It's really good for me to understand you in that broader context," or "That must have been difficult to share, but I appreciate you even more than before, because I know more about you now."

Carefully plan the next meeting with your friend. Look for an opportunity to share another low-risk item you have not previously shared with this person. If your friend follows up by sharing more, you should be prepared to affirm your friend and let him or her know a bit more about you.

You can share many safe things. Talk about your clothes, hobbies, or where you live. Speak about why you appreciate your friend, the kind of work you enjoy doing, or what you'd like to accomplish before you die. You can talk about some of your favorite leisure activities or what you like to read or watch on TV. There are hundreds of safe areas to talk about that will help your friend know more about you.

Everything you do or think in life has a reason behind it. Self-disclosure is your willingness to talk about the reasons behind what you think and do. Underline the last two sentences. They are the key concept to the meaning of self-disclosure.

Don't share with all of your friends at the same time or even during the same week. Practice growing in self-disclosure with only one friend at a time.

Remember that each person will differ in the ability to handle your self-disclosure. Some people will love it. They will want to know more about you and will reveal themselves to you. Other people will be frightened and immediately stop the process. It's okay for each person to relate to you at the depth that person chooses. What we are working toward is reducing your hesitancy to develop deeper friendships.

Realize that self-disclosure is not an end in itself. The purpose of sharing is to deepen friendship. Focusing on the relationship will keep you from being a self-disclosing exhibitionist. You're not trying to show off your insides or brag about your self-disclosure. You are quietly developing this ability so that you have stronger relationships, at various depths, with many people.

The following tips are meant to keep you from looking at self-disclosure as an end in itself.

Self-disclosure should not be a dramatic revelation of a secret sin. Disclosure should flow naturally and without stress for both of you. Self-disclosure should be part of the ongoing tendency of your relationship, not something that is dramatically done on occasion.

Self-disclosure should be a mutual experience. If you disclose more than your friend does, the result will likely be that your relationship will collapse. Keep it equal or seek a new friend.

Self-disclosure is best when it deals with the here and now. Yes, it is sometimes important to talk about how you feared your father as a child, but it would be more important to relate that old fact to today by sharing that you are still afraid of him. Don't keep bringing up past problems unless they relate to the present.

Your disclosures should not only be the negative side of your personality. Let your friend know about your strengths, joys, hopes, and aspirations. Give the full picture of who you see yourself to be. Try not to let false humility keep you from sharing the total you. Your friend does want to know you.

Self-disclose at all levels. There are three major avenues of self-disclosure that you'll use.

1. Words. Remember the sentences I asked you to underline? **Everything you do or think in life has a reason behind it. Self-**

disclosure is your willingness to talk about the reasons behind what you think and do. Self-disclosure is talking about the meaning behind your actions, ideas, and attitudes. Words are powerful and important tools, enabling your friend to know who you are. But remember, this is a gradual process.

Yesterday I walked along the beach with an old friend whom I hadn't seen for six years. Don and I caught up on what had been happening in our lives and what we have been thinking. I shared with him how tired I was of being liked because of what I do rather than for who I am.

My self-disclosure allowed each of us to talk more about what was going on in our lives. At the end of the afternoon when Don had to leave, he said, "I don't feel as if we've been as closely in touch as we ought to have been. I'm promising you I'm going to stay closer and develop our relationship."

I needed to hear that. It was like a good massage for my heart. But I don't think it ever would have happened unless I had been willing to be vulnerable about who I am now.

2. Body. Earlier we talked about the skill of attending. Your body communicates information about you. Use nonverbal expressions as another means of disclosing who you are.

The tone of your voice, the speed, inflection, and intensity of your words, the amount of eye contact, your facial expression, the way you're sitting or standing—all communicate something about you.

A powerful way to use your nonverbals is to link them with verbal expressions. For example, suppose your friend suggests, "Why don't we get together on Monday for lunch?" You're hesitant because you don't have the time on Monday. You will probably respond with a hesitancy shown by the speed of your words, the tone of your voice, and your facial expression.

In the past you might have used evasive words such as, "I don't think I can make it." Your friend certainly would spot your hesitancy. Instead, take the opportunity to say to your friend, "I want to be with you very much. My hesitancy is that Monday is a very busy day for me. Could we meet Friday instead?"

3. Values. Every action of your life has a value behind it. Sensitive and insightful people will observe your actions and begin to piece together the kinds of things you value.

Don't make friends guess about your meanings and values. Tell them what your actions mean. Tell them why you work where you do, why you choose certain friends, the car you drive, the place you live, the church you attend, the political stands you take, and so on. Talk about the meanings behind each of these actions and decisions.

Practice Your New Skill

Change comes about because you are dissatisfied with things as they are. Practicing new actions or attitudes will help to cement a new lifestyle or thinking process.

The growth activities in the last section of the chapter are not an option. You need to rehearse them so that self-disclosure becomes a natural part of your lifestyle. Following are some suggestions for your practice. I hope that by now you are, on your own, thinking of creative ways to integrate this skill into your personality.

Individual Growth Activities

1. What subjects about yourself are the most difficult for you to share? (Examples: money, sex, power, personal weakness, or your family background.)
2. Ask yourself, for each area, what would happen if you shared in this area with a friend. (Think of "worst possible" and "best possible" scenarios.)

3. Now carefully plan to risk by sharing one of the difficult areas of your life with a friend with whom you have a trusting relationship.

Group Growth Activities

Have a group "What would you do" session. Each person is to suggest a situational question that would require some personal revelation, and all other members are to respond. Example: "What would you do if ..."

- your powerful boss at work unfairly criticized your friend?
- a friend wanted to borrow $3,000?
- you were offered more money at a job requiring a move to another state?
- your mother wanted to live with you permanently?

Chapter 12

Skill #6

Affirmation: Passing On a Blessing

My Uncle Art, a pastor, taught me a lot about preaching. In fact, I learned more from him about the preparation and delivery of a sermon than I did in any of my seminary training.

After he had heard me speak on one occasion he said, "You remind me of myself during my early days of preaching." He described his preaching style as "people-clubbing." He explained, "I carried two clubs into the pulpit. I'd knock the people down with the club in one hand, and when they got up, I'd hit them with the club in my other hand."

Uncle Art advised, "If you want to be an effective pastor, you have to be more than a prophet who points out people's sins. You also need to be their friend." His comment made such a strong impact on me that I began to listen to myself as I preached. I decided I'd better put away my clubs.

On one occasion I told the people in my congregation, "I really like you. I am thankful you are people who are serious about God, who believe in prayer, who are concerned about people, and who love me and my family." I went on to say, "I'm grateful for my position as your pastor, because I'm doing exactly what I want to do, and on top of all this, you pay me for it."

I hadn't planned to include those comments in my message, but after the service I was fascinated by the warm response from the people. The affirmation I had given from the pulpit caused them to be warmer to me as well as to each other.

I had known before that people in counseling sessions responded well to affirmation, but this was the first time I had clearly expressed affirmation to the congregation from the pulpit. That incident, and my uncle's comments, helped me begin to affirm people regularly as I preached.

In this chapter we'll think about how to develop this skill of affirmation, or "passing on a blessing." We'll consider what this skill is, why it is important, factors that may keep you from affirming your friends, and finally, specific ways to develop this skill.

What Is Affirmation?

In its simplest form, affirmation is identifying some characteristic, trait, or action in another person and giving praise for that quality or action. Many times affirmation is passed between people without a conscious realization they are affirming each other. Still, I want you to understand affirmation so thoroughly that you can intentionally affirm your friends. Let's focus now on what affirmation is.

Enabling. Affirmation is related to the concept of "enabling" that we touched on earlier. Affirmation is, first of all, understanding your friend's potential. Affirming then becomes a process of encouragement which moves your friend to use all of his or her resources to arrive at the highest level of productivity and creativity.

Warmth. A technical description for affirmation is "nonpossessive warmth." Carl Rogers says that in nonpossessive warmth one communicates a "deep and genuine caring for him as a person with potential, a caring uncontaminated by evaluation of his thoughts, feelings, or behaviors."[1]

Affirmation is not for manipulation; instead, you identify qualities, traits, and potential within a person that you want to warmly encourage.

A personal gift. Affirmation might also be described as a gift that every human being needs to become a true human being. Three minutes of affirmation a day properly given by a father to his son will be worth more than providing eighteen years of food, clothing, shelter, medical care, and education.

Rachel was a new Christian. She grew up in a home where she received no affirmation. She felt insecure as a person, as a student, and as a woman. She said to me, "I feel as if my skin doesn't fit." She felt as if there wasn't enough person inside to fill out her body. Rachel felt like a hollow shell.

In one session, while talking about her parents, she said, "I just want them to love me—to tell me **one time** they love me. I want them to say that they are glad for anything that I am doing. If my father would just hold me in his arms and tell me that he loves me—I feel I could be a real person and get on with my life."

Affirmation is more than just words. It has the dimensions of touch, tone, and caring—a deep, loving desire for the other person. As you understand its indispensableness, you'll realize that affirmation is not an optional skill. Yes, you can choose to affirm or withhold, but no genuine friendship exists without affirmation flowing between the friends.

Giving. In a marvelous book entitled *The Blessing,* Gary Smalley and John Trent enrich our understanding of affirmation. They outline five different ways to bless another person's life:

- meaningful touch
- spoken message
- attaching "high value" to the one being blessed
- picturing a special future for the one being blessed
- an active commitment to fulfill the blessing[2]

These key concepts point out that true affirmation has the dimension of giving. Giving is hard to do, however, if your bank is empty.

I became a Christian just before I went to college. I was insecure, a poor student, and broke. I remember the first time I read Luke 6, which discusses loving your enemies, turning the cheek, and going the second mile. I was grabbed by these verses: "If you love those who love you, what credit is that to you? For even sinners love those who love them.... And if you lend to those from whom you expect to receive, what credit is that to you? ... But love your enemies, and do good, and lend, expecting nothing in return."[3]

Because I had little to give emotionally and financially, I tightly held on to everything I had. It was difficult for me to give something away and not expect a return. That's one of the reasons I found it difficult to affirm people. I felt if I gave them encouragement, their lives would progress and I would be left even further behind in the dust.

Many people who have trouble affirming others are themselves insecure and need to be affirmed. It's a vicious circle. They would affirm, if only they were affirmed. They would be glad to pass on a blessing if only they had a blessing to pass on.

By now you're beginning to get the picture. I hope you understand why in the beginning I talked so extensively about your own personal life and attitudes. If you feel insecure, you are likely to have difficulty practicing affirmation.

Don't throw in the towel, though. Remember: We're not

expecting perfection. You can grow so that you are comfortable being a friend. If you feel inadequate about giving affirmation, don't worry. We'll walk through a training process later in this chapter to develop this skill.

Receiving. I have described and defined affirmation in several ways. Now I want to add one more dimension that may seem strange, but it is part of applying affirmation to friendship. Affirmation has the dimension of receiving. It works this way. Suppose you affirm your friend, but your friend doesn't receive it. The person brushes it off and rejects it. Your affirmation is like water running off a duck's back.

I have a friend who fidgets when I begin to give affirmation. He starts to talk loudly, right over the top of what I'm trying to say, as if to drown out my affirmation. Strangely, at the same time, he has a smile on his face.

The smile says to me, "I really like what you're saying." But the agitation and the excited talking says, "My bad self-image rejects what you're saying."

You can help your friend be more open to receiving affirmation by your own attitude of freely accepting affirmation. The appropriate way to handle affirmation is to look at the person, smile gently, and say, "Thank you, I really appreciate that," or "That certainly feels good, especially coming from a trusted friend like you."

Notice, you did not go through the denial routine or the false humility. Rather, you believed what your friend was saying and thanked him. It's possible for you to accept your friend's affirmation and at the same time to pass a blessing to that person by calling him a "trusted friend."

When you reject someone's affirmation of you, you may be saying, in effect, "I'm not sure if you are lying, trying to manipulate me, or have some kind of distorted view of me." Those are not positive inferences to suggest to your friend. If, on the other hand, you accept the affirmation without negative disclaimers, your friend will automatically feel good about himself.

Sometimes the rejection of affirmation is really a cover-up for pride. We are too proud to let our friend know how much we crave to be affirmed, so the false humility ploy of saying, "Oh, that's not true," is used as a camouflage. It would be better to say, "Thank you. I really appreciate that encouragement, especially from a valued friend like you."

The Importance of Affirmation

Following are several important benefits resulting from your affirmation of your friend.

Affirmation reduces defensiveness. If your friend sees that you value and appreciate her, that person doesn't have to be defensive around you. Affirmation helps your friend trust you and reduces the fear of being judged.

It's true that some people use affirmation to soften up people, and then they slap them with a truly critical comment. But when you give affirmation and don't follow it up with a kick in the pants, your friend will be less wary of you and his defenses will be lowered.

Affirmation encourages sharing. After a person is affirmed, the almost involuntary response is to pass the affirmation back to the person who started the affirming. Affirmation brings a new openness, a new capacity to share and trust. The result is a new desire for mutual affirmation and mutual sharing of lives.

Affirmation refocuses problems. Ben and Martha had a teenage son who was more interested in hanging around with a tough group of high-school boys than the local Campus Life group. In one of the adult Sunday-school classes on parenting, Martha was confronted with the reality that she loved her boy to a degree, but she didn't love and affirm him in the way he needed.

She decided to demonstrate her love for her son by reaching out and loving his friends.

That change of thinking in Martha started a whole series of encouraging events. Their home became an open meeting place for their son and his friends. The ultimate result was that several of the high-school friends became Christians, and Ben and Martha moved into a deep adult friendship with their son. As you begin to affirm people, you will notice that many of the problems you thought you had with them will become smaller or even nonexistent.

Affirmation increases productivity. Ted Engstrom shares this story:

> Years ago there was a group of brilliant young men at the University of Wisconsin who seemed to have amazing creative literary talent. They were would-be poets, novelists, and essayists. They were extraordinary in their ability to put the English language to its best use. These promising young men met regularly to read and critique each other's work. And critique it they did! . . .
>
> They were heartless, tough, even mean in their criticism. The sessions became such arenas of literary criticism that the members of this exclusive club called themselves the "Stranglers."

Interestingly, women at the University of Wisconsin who also had literary talent started their own club.

> They called themselves the "Wranglers." They, too, read their works to one another. But there was one great difference. The criticism was much softer, more positive, more encouraging. Sometimes there was almost no criticism at all. Every effort, even the most feeble one, was encouraged.
>
> Twenty years later an alumnus of the university was doing an exhaustive study of his classmates' careers when he noticed a vast difference in the literary accomplishments of the Stranglers as opposed to the Wranglers. Of all of the bright young men in the Stranglers, not one had made a significant literary accomplishment of any kind. From the Wranglers had come six or more successful

writers, some of national renown such as Marjorie Kinnan Rawlings who wrote *The Yearling*."[4]

Sometimes people believe it is their role in life to confront and correct people. There **are** rare times for that. But positive affirmation will more often help a friend move in the right direction than will confrontation.

Affirmation provides perspective. None of us has an accurate picture of who we are as individuals. We need the insights of other people. You can do a great service for your friends by identifying the strengths you see in them.

Most people are more aware of their weaknesses than they are their strengths. As you affirm your friends, you give them a balanced perspective on who they are in positive ways and what they have to offer to society.

Affirmation provides motivation. I have watched the effect of affirmation change me a thousand times. As I am affirmed, I experience an involuntary response that makes me want to continue doing the thing for which I was affirmed.

You probably experienced this as a child. When a parent, relative, or teacher affirmed you for the great job you were doing, you wanted to do it again. We are automatically drawn to those activities and people that give us loving affirmation.

It happened to me again yesterday. A long-distance call came from a young woman who was a teenager when I was pastoring Twin City Bible Church in Urbana, Illinois. She was at the point of tears, needing some help and perspective in her life. We talked for half-an-hour. She seemed to get some direction and felt relieved. She said, "I'm glad you're such an understanding person. I'm glad you didn't put me down or make me feel inadequate. Most of all, I'm glad you were willing to talk to me in the middle of your busy schedule."

When I hung up the phone, I felt so good I wanted to help

somebody else. I was emotionally up the rest of the day. Her affirmation made me want to continue helping people.

Affirmation models the life of Christ. Jesus repeatedly lifted people to higher levels of achievement and self-perception because of his affirmation. The disciples were men whose lives were changed because of Christ's confidence in them. Zaccheus, the woman at the well, and many other individuals grew because of affirmation from Jesus. They immediately reacted differently to their life situations and to the people around them because they believed Jesus' affirmations of them and their futures.

Factors That Limit Affirmation

Several things might keep you from affirming your friend. I'll only point out a few of the more significant factors.

First, your family life and past experience may not have equipped you to affirm people spontaneously. If you were not affirmed in the past, you will need to practice the skill until it becomes a natural part of you. The Bible reminds us that the failures of the fathers can be passed down through several generations.[5]

If you have not been affirmed by your parents, you are not likely to affirm your children, who in turn are not likely to be affirming people. **Somewhere, someone must break that cycle!** I pray that you will take the initiative to break that cycle and become an affirming person. Your change of direction will affect generations to come.

A second factor that will limit your affirmation is an unwillingness to forgive. I think of a couple who were having marital problems. Eventually the wife got involved with another man. Her husband, however, did not know about the affair. Finally, through counseling, Susan came to the point where she was willing to break off the affair and work on her marriage.

As part of reestablishing her marriage, she wanted to tell her husband, John, about her affair so that they could start with a clean slate. When she asked for forgiveness, John grudgingly granted her partial forgiveness.

For several weeks I encouraged him to forgive his wife totally. When we got down to the core of the issue, two factors were keeping him from forgiving his wife. He felt she had not fully paid for her sin, and he was tormented by the thought of his wife with another man. To put it in his words, "She can waltz into the living room and ask for my forgiveness and be a free woman. I am the one who pays the price. I'm the one being punished."

By not forgiving her, John was continuing to punish her for what she had done. He was unwilling to forgive Susan because he wanted to control her. He wanted to keep her from getting involved in another affair. He felt insecure because she was a very sensuous woman. Since he thought little of himself, he was sure that she might easily be attracted to "better" men.

The tragedy of John's unforgiveness was that he was not punishing Susan but himself. Neither was he controlling his wife; he was only driving her away. The marriage continued to deteriorate until they were finally divorced.

If your friend violates you in some way and asks for your forgiveness, you must fully and freely forgive. A request for forgiveness is also a good opportunity to affirm the person. You might say, "Mary, I'm so glad we talked about this. I'm glad for your bravery in asking for forgiveness. Of course, I forgive you. I love you even more because you are an up-front person who wants to have an open relationship with me." Now Mary feels good because she is forgiven and has been told she is an open person.

A third common factor limiting affirmation is competition. Have you ever noticed junior-high-school girls? Attractive girls frequently hang around with unattractive girls. They are insecure and need each other. The attractive girl needs the less attractive one to provide contrast to make her look better. The unattractive girl draws vicariously from the attractive girl and her circle of friends. While they both need each other, the relationship is one of desperate competition.

When you compete with your friend, you may have a subconscious desire to cut that person down rather than to affirm. Competition may unconsciously cause you to overlook the positive that could be affirmed in your friend. In the short run, putting your friend down may make you look good, but ultimately it will cause you to lose your friendship.

When I find myself thinking competitively toward other people, it's helpful for me to think of Jesus as my model. He was "gentle and humble in heart."[6] He was willing to humble himself, become a man, and die for us. As I pattern my life after him, my competition with others begins to be diffused.

Recently I struggled with competitive thoughts toward some of my famous friends who seem to be accomplishing much more than I. Sally pulled me back to reality by reminding me of Philippians 4: "Finally, brethren, whatever is true, whatever is honorable, whatever is right, whatever is pure, whatever is lovely, whatever is of good repute, if there is any excellence and if anything worthy of praise, let your mind dwell on these things."[7]

I found it helpful to thank God for the good things I see in the lives of people with whom I feel competitive. As I thanked God, my life came into better perspective. I was more content to keep doing what God has asked me to do and be genuinely grateful that my famous friends are succeeding. I could sincerely say to one the next time I saw him, "I'm so glad for the contribution you are making in our Christian culture today."

When you affirm someone, it appears on the surface that you are losing something of yourself to another person. Your initial subconscious thought may be, "I'm giving myself away. This person will get ahead of me." The end result, however, is that mutual giving is created.

How to Develop the Skill of Affirmation

Know your friend. For your affirmation to be effective, you can't just shoot in the dark. You must understand your friend's needs.

For example, you might say to me, "You've done a nice job washing your car." That could be an accurate statement, but since washing the car is not a high value in my life, your affirmation would not make much of an impact on me.

On the other hand, if you say to me that I have done a good job writing this book and it has touched your life so that your relationships are changed, you will have affirmed me in a crucial value area of my life.

To know your friend, you have to get into his or her world. You need to see through your friend's eyes and understand life as that person understands it.

> To care for another person, I must be able to understand him and his world as if I were inside it. I must be able to see, as it were, with his eyes what his world is like to him and how he sees himself. Instead of merely looking at him in a detached way from outside, as if he were a specimen, I must be able to be **with** him in his world, "going" into his world in order to sense from the "inside" what life is like for him, what he is striving to be and what he requires to grow.[8]

Obviously, all of the attitudes and the skills we've discussed are going to be very important as you come to understand your friend deeply. Give yourself some time to put all the pieces of information together so that your affirmations are really on target.

It might be helpful to use the following list to help you understand your friend. List the following:

- six activities that bring happiness to your friend
- concerns that make your friend angry
- half a dozen of your friend's skills or talents
- other friends who are important to your friend
- three of your friend's most frequent daydreams
- what your friend would do if he or she could do anything
- three things your friend wants to accomplish before death
- the status of your friend's personal relationship to God

These starter ideas should help you get a view of your friend from the inside out, rather than just looking from the outside in.

Focus on positives rather than negatives. Sometimes people who want to affirm another person say to themselves, "I need to straighten out my friend so that she doesn't continue to do the same dumb thing."

Their concern is one of love and a deep desire to help. Unfortunately, focusing only on negatives and criticism puts distance between people. Now don't get me wrong. There is a time for confrontation, but whenever it is done, you must realize that you are going to lose ground in the friendship. **Distance will be created!**

I hope your friendship is strong enough so that the distance can be closed up and result in growth. But there is always a risk when criticism is used. Positive affirmation can accomplish much of the same growth and development in your friend without the lost ground caused by criticism.

The Bible says, "We love [God] because he first loved us."[9] We don't love God because he slaps us, kicks us around, makes us feel cheap, inadequate, stupid, and insignificant. We probably feel some of those things about ourselves already. We love God because—in spite of what we might feel about ourselves—he loves and accepts us. He has a positive future in mind for us.

"'Cheer up, don't be afraid. For the Lord your God has

arrived to live among you. He is the mighty Savior. He will give you victory. He will rejoice over you in great gladness; He will love you and not accuse you.' Is that a joyous choir I hear? No, it is the Lord Himself exalting over you in happy song."[10] Be a godlike positive affirmer for your friend.

Affirm differences. One of the important lessons I learned while I was pastor at Newton Bible Church, Newton, Kansas, was to appreciate a different point of view and to affirm that difference.

The church was led by the board of deacons, which like any board had people who held differing viewpoints. As issues were discussed, frequently a majority and a minority viewpoint would develop. The typical solution to this problem in many organizations is to vote on it. The result is that the minority always loses, because the majority has more votes.

Again and again, I watched how these deacons handled their differing opinions. Invariably, after thorough discussion, the man who held the minority view would move that we adopt the majority view. He wasn't being voted down. He was recognizing the will of the group and the leading of God.

After the motion then passed unanimously, the men who held the majority view would affirm the man who had held the minority view and who brought about unity by moving that the majority view be adopted. The majority also acknowledged that the man with the minority view had an important point that needed to be remembered as the group carried out the motion.

Don't be put off by your friend's different viewpoints. Those differences can add to your life. You will have a broader perspective as you appreciate and affirm differences in your friend.

Choose to affirm small areas frequently rather than large areas occasionally. The next time you have a contact with your friend, try verbal affirmation at least three times. Comment on your friend's smile, clothes, tan, or weight loss. Don't save all of your affirmation for one blowout on your friend's birthday.

Earlier I cautioned you to affirm your friend in the important areas of life. Don't let my warning intimidate you so that you don't affirm at all until you have found the **most** important area of your friend's life. Your affirmation will be more on target, however, as you affirm the areas that are most valued by your friend.

Touch. Affirmation is also communicated by your touch. As you greet your friend, use touch to show that you're glad to be there.

Our culture has some unwritten codes about acceptable ways and times of touching. For example, if you are a man meeting another man with whom you have a beginning friendship, shaking hands would be appropriate. If you follow that up by putting your left hand on your new friend's forearm, elbow, or shoulder while you shake hands, you will indicate to your friend that he is more than just a handshake friend. He is special. A bear hug, however, might not be appropriate until you know each other better.

Be sensitive to how much and what kind of touch is suitable. The depth of your relationship, the occasion, and the sex of your friend all have a part in the kind of touching you should do. Our Christian culture has become much more touch-oriented in recent decades. In fact, not to touch can come across as cold and aloof. If you're not sure about what kind of touching is appropriate at first, at least reach out to touch your friend's hand.

Touch has a profound effect on people. A study done at the library of Purdue University demonstrated that you can change the attitudes of people through touch. Librarians were asked to touch the hands of certain students as they handed them books or their library cards. The results showed that students who were touched had a more positive attitude about the library and the librarians than did the students who were not touched.[11]

Marilyn Monroe was asked one time by a *New York Times* reporter, "Did you ever feel loved by any of the foster families with whom you lived?" "Once, when I was about 7 or 8. The woman I was living with was putting on make-up, and I was watching her. . . . She reached over and patted my cheeks with her rouge puff, . . . for that moment, I felt loved by her."[12]

It was only the touch of a rouge puff, but it lasted for years. Don't underestimate the impact or the longevity of your touch.

A number of times I have visited people in the hospital who are unconscious. My mind tells me it is a waste of time to go into the room, because that person won't even know I am there.

On one occasion I visited Donna, who had been thrown from a horse and was unconscious for days. I went to the hospital to visit the family, but they had stepped out for a while. I went on into Donna's room, deciding I could at least pray over her.

She was motionless in her bed with tubes and wires running in and out of her body. I spoke to her, but there was no response. As I reached down and took hold of Donna's hand, I noticed a slight fluttering of her eyelids. I held her hand and quoted a section of Scripture. Then I prayed that God would heal her and restore her to her family.

Some weeks later, after Donna had regained consciousness, she shared with me that she knew I was there that day and desperately wanted to thank me for holding her hand and praying. At the time she was unable to let me know that she knew.

Your touch on the shoulder, pat on the back, or firm, prolonged handshake will tell your friend that you care.

The Practical Procedure

Okay, now let's do it. You're going to be with your friend in the next day or so and you want to be able to give affirmation.

1. Go back and skim chapter 3, "Why We Like People, Why They Like Us," and chapter 6, "Qualities That Build Friendships." Remember, focusing on your friend is one way of affirming. The ideas that we walked through in those two chapters are going to help you focus on your friend. Automatically your friend will feel affirmed.

2. Put your **attending** skills to work. **Look** at your friend. Sit or stand near your friend. Focus your body and your attention fully on that person.

3. Use your **listening** and **empathy** skills as your friend shares what's been happening in his or her life. Your caring will help your friend to feel affirmed.

Notice that you haven't done any talking yet. You are just using some of your friendship skills to help that other person feel special.

4. Before you meet, spend time thinking about who your friend is as a person. Identify areas to verbally affirm.

5. Greet your friend with a warm smile. Look directly into his or her face. Appropriately touch your friend and follow up with a verbal affirmation such as, "I'm so glad we have this time to be together," "You are one of the people I count as an important friend in my life."

6. Now as your friend speaks, listen empathetically. When you respond, be open and real. Look for opportunities to affirm your friend with a smile, a spoken word, or an appropriate touch. Always focus on who that person is in his or her inner being.

Gayle Erwin, in his book *The Jesus Style,* tells the story of his father's funeral, which aptly illustrates the impact of affirmation.

> When my father died, my two brothers and I stood in front of his casket and made the following statement to the friends who had gathered for the funeral service; "Our father did not leave a financial empire for us to carry on. Many things that a dad normally does with his sons, ours was unable to do. He was unable

to teach us many things that a dad normally teaches. But he did leave us something that he had. He left us with a love of God, a love for the Bible, a love of people, an understanding of worship and an inability to hate. We feel that he has left us only those things that will last. So we stand before you as his sons and declare publicly that we will follow his God."[13]

As you affirm your friends, they will be forever changed. Affirming people will draw them to you and they will long remember your loving, outspoken appreciation of them.

Individual Growth Activities

For the next week, commit yourself to affirm someone before you allow yourself to eat each meal. Build up someone's self-worth by encouraging that person's decisions, goals, actions, or personal characteristics. Keep a running list of the people you have affirmed, how you affirmed them, and their reaction.

Group Growth Activities

1. Group members should verbally affirm another member in the group while maintaining strong eye contact. The affirmed person must respond with an acceptance of the affirmation such as, "Thank you, I really needed that." Continue around the group so that each person is affirmed once before anyone is affirmed twice.
2. Have the group members form a circle. One person takes a ball of yarn and, while grasping one end of the yarn, throws the ball across the circle to someone. As the first person throws the yarn ball, he or she says something to affirm the receiver.

    The receiver then grasps the yarn strand at the edge of the ball and throws the ball to someone else while giving that person some words of affirmation. Continue throwing the ball from person to person with each thrower giving affirmation to each receiver. As the yarn ball is tossed from person to person, the strands of yarn will crisscross the room.

After everyone has received the ball one time, the ball may be thrown to people for second and third turns. The network of yarn from person to person will visually demonstrate your connectedness.

Part Four

LIFE APPLICATION

Chapter 13

Putting It All Together

When I come to the end of a book I have really enjoyed, I have mixed feelings. I feel melancholic. I don't want it to end. I've come to know the author, and I've wrestled with new ideas, as well as with my own feelings. I want that dialogue with the author to continue.

I also feel reflective. I review how I've grown. I think about where I'm going in my life, and I'm eager to try out my new ideas.

Ending a book is like moving to a new neighborhood. Whenever I've moved, I've felt sad about leaving old friends and familiar surroundings that have provided me security and peace. At the same time, I've felt eager to get acquainted with the new house, neighbors, and community. I've felt a sense of challenge. I've expected things to be better.

Sigmund Freud believed that most of our life is controlled by the things that happened in our past, especially in our very early childhood. His student Carl Jung, however, taught that humans are controlled by the pull of their future as well as by their past.

The purpose of this chapter is to encourage you to reflect a little on your past—what we have been doing together. But I also want you to feel the **tug of the future.** What's going to happen now? Who are you becoming? Who will you become in your relationships?

Ask yourself, "Am I becoming a more real person? Am I becoming a lover of people—a servant? Are my relationships built on understanding and enriching other people's lives, or are they focused too much on me and my desperate sense of loneliness?" Or ask these questions another way, "Am I becoming a **real** friend?"

There's a fascinating children's story called *The Velveteen Rabbit.* The rabbit came to the little boy's house as a present one Christmas morning. For a few hours the rabbit was really loved by the little boy, until the boy became preoccupied with other toys and activities. After Christmas the rabbit was just one of the many toys in the toy cupboard. He felt very insignificant and common.

One day the Velveteen Rabbit was thrown into a pile right next to the Skin Horse, who was very old and wise. The Horse had survived, even though tattered, while a succession of mechanical toys had come and gone.

"What is **REAL?**" asked the Rabbit one day, when they were lying side by side. "Does it mean having things that buzz inside you and a stick-out handle?"

"Real isn't how you are made," said the Skin Horse. "It's a thing that happens to you. When a child loves you for a long, long time, not just to play with, but **REALLY** loves you, then you become Real."

"Does it happen all at once, like being wound up," he asked, "or bit by bit?"

"It doesn't happen all at once," said the Skin Horse. "You

become. It takes a long time. That's why it doesn't often happen to people who break easily, or have sharp edges, or who have to be carefully kept. Generally, by the time you are Real, most of your hair has been loved off, and your eyes drop out and you get loose in the joints and very shabby. But these things don't matter at all, because once you are Real you can't be ugly, except to people who don't understand."[1]

Time went by and almost by accident, the little boy's "Nana" put the Velveteen Rabbit in bed with him one night. For many nights following, the little boy slept with the Rabbit. The Rabbit liked being the boy's friend and sharing all of the boy's stories, adventures, and tears. Sometimes it was hard for the Rabbit, because he would get hugged very tightly or almost get smashed as the boy rolled around in his sleep.

Time passed and the Rabbit was happy. He never noticed that his velveteen fur was getting shabby and his tail was coming loose because the boy hugged him so much.

A wonderful, close relationship developed between the boy and the Rabbit. But one spring as the boy was playing make-believe adventures with his Rabbit out in the yard, the boy was suddenly called away. Unfortunately, he left the little Rabbit outside.

That evening the boy missed his Rabbit and asked his "Nana" to go outside and find him. She found the Rabbit, but he was soaked with dew. Grumbling, she brought him back into the house and tried to clean him up with the end of her apron. "You must have your old Bunny!" she said. "Fancy all that fuss for a toy!" The boy sat up in bed and stretched out his hands. "Give me my Bunny!" he said. "You mustn't say that. He isn't a toy. He's **REAL!**"[2]

That's it, that's what happens between kids and their toys. Magically they make them into real live beings. The Velveteen Rabbit had suddenly become **REAL!**

The same can happen with people. As you understand people, serve them, meet their needs, and use your friendship skills to enrich them, you will change them from being just another person among the world's billions to that magical and wonderful entity called "friend."

Friendship—that's what we've been working toward in this book. I really want you to develop a spontaneous **lifestyle of friendship.**

Let's consider how you can sustain these friendship skills for the rest of your life. The likelihood of a long-term lifestyle of friendship can be increased by looking at three major areas:

1. **Review what you have learned**
2. **Spontaneously sustain relationships**
3. **Reproduce your experience**

Review What You Have Learned

Reviewing takes only a few minutes, but the material you review will last. Much of what we read only one time washes out of our brain. Reviewing, jotting notes to yourself, or working on projects will cement your learning. Use the following questions to guide your cementing process.

Chapter 1: Listen to Me

What did you think or feel as I shared some of my life and background with you? Were you reminded of your difficult or successful times as a child? Did your successes or failures influence your friendships? (Try to give a concrete answer to each question.)

Chapter 2: This Is Going to Be Fun!

What did you think and feel as I encouraged you to forget past failures with friendships? Did you notice any correlation between your friendships with people and your relationship with God? Did you feel uncomfortable or encouraged when I suggested that you didn't need to be friends with everyone?

Chapter 3: Why We Like People, Why They Like Us

What things came to your mind about other people or yourself when we thought about various traits or attitudes that cause people to like or not like each other? What changes did you resolve to make in your own life?

Chapter 4: What Do I Think of Myself?

What did you think of yourself when you started reading the book? What do you think of yourself now? What were the forces that formed you as a person? Has perfectionism held you back?

Chapter 5: The Maturing Person

I asked you to make several lists. What kind of person did you discover yourself to be? Did you decide on new directions for your life? Did you decide to courageously be yourself? In what areas?

Chapter 6: Qualities That Build Friendships

We thought together about some of the qualities that helped friendships work, such as being nonjudgmental, accepting, genuine, self-disclosing, caring, committed, enabling, firm, and spiritually concerned. How did you stack up in those areas? Remember, we were not looking for perfection; we were looking for progress, growth, and improvement.

Chapter 7: Attending: Focusing on Your Friend

We thought together about how to pay attention to another person with your whole body and mind. Think for a moment about how you have changed. In what ways have your attending skills improved so that you effectively focus on your friend? (At each chapter review, look away from the book and reflect on what you have read.)

Chapter 8: Listening: One Part of Communication

How much did your listening skills improve? What happened as you started to listen creatively and more carefully to people? How have your friends responded to you?

Chapter 9: Talking: Another Part of Communication

How have your attitudes changed about talking? Which skills and friendship qualities have most contributed to changing your attitudes toward the talking side of communication?

Chapter 10: Empathy: Caring Enough to Send Your Very Best

Think back over the development of your empathy. Notice how much more sensitive you are to people's feelings rather than to their ideas alone. What projects most helped you to develop your skill?

Chapter 11: Genuineness: Being Real in a Phony World

In what ways are you more open with people? How has openness deepened your relationships?

Chapter 12: Affirmation: Passing On a Blessing

How have people reacted to your affirmation of them? How have you felt as you affirmed people?

As you carefully think over each area of growth and development in your life, you are reinforcing and sustaining what you have learned. Sometimes the temptation while reading a book such as this one is to skip over the review. The purpose of the review is to reinforce and permanently cement ideas and experiences into your life.

If you found yourself rushing through that review, go over it again. Perhaps this time you could make notes on 3x5 cards. Tape one card a day on your bathroom mirror. Each morning as you get ready for the day, think through your changing attitudes and skills.

Spontaneously Sustain Relationships

The basic question now is, "How do we sustain what we have learned?"

Our youngest daughter, Becki, at the end of her college training, did an internship at a care facility for brain-injured people. Many of the patients were men who had been injured in motorcycle accidents and functioned at a very low level.

The center had to train some of the men to repeatedly check their shirt pockets for a cue card prepared by the staff. The cue card reminded each man what he was supposed to be doing at that time. The card might remind him that he was eating, playing a game, or dressing. Tragically, these men were not able to function spontaneously. They had to be reminded of the very activities in which they were currently engaged.

I'm not suggesting that you go around with friendship cue cards in your pockets, reminding you to be a friend, but your cards on the mirror may reinforce your growth. Friendship building will become an increasingly natural part of your personality as you integrate these skills into your life.

Let's boil this book down to two basic concepts and the activities that should result.

1. Understand People. As you think over the attitudes, qualities, and skills of friendship, you will notice that I've been pushing you to understand people. People are crying out to be understood and every true friendship is made up of a deep and accurate understanding between people.

You will spontaneously maintain relationships as you continue to refine your skills toward a more complete understanding of people.

2. Serve People. Exploiters are shunned by people. But people who serve, without being required to do so, automatically win friends.

Just before Jesus went to the Garden of Gethsemane and eventually to the Cross, he met with his disciples in the Upper Room. In Bible times, it was customary as a visitor entered a home to have a servant remove his street sandals, bathe his feet, and put on indoor slippers.

No servants were present, and the disciples were so busy competing with each other that certainly none of them was going to serve the others by washing feet. If one of them had washed the others' feet, he would definitely have been viewed as a servant, not an equal.

During the dinner Jesus got up from the table, took off his robes, put on a towel, and started to wash each man's feet. They then recognized how wrong they had been. Greatness is not achieved through competition or force, but through service. Jesus not only modeled service but also told them that they were to serve each other as the normal pattern of life.[3]

It's not just a Christian principle; it's a human principle. We are drawn to people who understand us and who want to do things for us.

Your friendship skills are powerful tools. If they are used inappropriately, they can become manipulation to accomplish your selfish ends. If, however, the skills that you've learned are focused on the other person's nourishment and good, the tools will bring true friendship.

Now let's combine these two principles into one major thrust:

Focus your energies and skills outwardly toward other people rather than inwardly on your personal needs.

The serendipitous or unplanned result will be that people will want to be your friends. You will be the kind of person others can trust to understand, nourish, and help them become all that they can be. You will find that people will spontaneously seek you out for friendship.

Reproduce Your Experience

The purpose of this chapter is to help you sustain what you've already learned. You will retain concepts and skills better if you teach or share them with another person.

As you were reading through the book and practicing your skills, you may have been identifying some of the people with whom you would like to share these ideas and skills. That's the beginning. You're on your way.

Teaching or sharing what you have learned will accomplish two goals at one time. You will enrich the life of your friend— and that's what friendship is all about—plus, you will firmly cement these friendship skills and attitudes into your personality.

I want to walk you through this exhilarating process of sharing what you've learned with another person or a small group of people. The coaching that I'll give you will apply to sharing with one person or a small group of four to eight people.

Let's divide it up into some convenient chunks, such as how to get started, covenants or agreements, structures that will take away the guesswork, possible problems, and finally, the future.

How to Get Started

Think of two or three people who have the following qualifications:

1. You have some degree of relationship with them
2. You want to get to know them better
3. They would benefit from learning these skills and attitudes

After you have identified these people, plan to use the next two to four weeks to find one of these friends to become a partner with you in sharing these skills and attitudes with a group of four to eight other friends. Ask God to help you identify that special person.

Now approach your potential partners one by one and share all of the information that appears in the next few pages. You will want your friends to be able to make a yes-or-no decision on the basis of full information.

You might say, "I have been reading a book that's really been a help to me. I was wondering if you would be willing to look over this book and perhaps the two of us could start a small group to discuss the ideas in it. We could meet with a group of four to eight other people before we go to work on Thursday mornings at six-thirty for about an hour. It looks as if it would take us about ten to fifteen weeks to get through the book. In the process of sharing, we would get to know each other better and develop our abilities to become friends with other people."

It's important that your friends understand fully what is involved in starting the group so that they can make an intelligent decision. If the first friend does not feel comfortable after looking over the book, go to the next person on your list. Give that one a book and share what you would like to accomplish. When you get your first person committed, you are on your way.

The two of you should then make a list of eight to twelve additional people who might be a potential group in this learning experience. Follow the same approach you did with your first friend. Give each person a few days to prayerfully consider a decision to join you in this adventure. For this group to be effective, it must be kept at a relatively small number, four to eight. Usually you will have to ask more people than the number with which you will actually end up. But soon you will have your group rounded up.

Covenants

Carefully think through what you are going to do as a group so that everyone knows exactly what to expect and can agree to the process. It's helpful to actually write out covenants, or agreements, so that everything is up-front about what is expected.

A preliminary covenant should be drawn up by you and your first friend. Then as you recruit people, you can intelligently tell them what's going to happen. At your very first meeting of the whole group, go over the covenant agreements in detail so that everyone has opportunity for input. Each person should fully agree with the covenant so that everyone feels that the words and ideas are their own.

A covenant should cover the following areas:

- where to meet
- time
- day of the week
- length of each get-together
- content to be covered
- goals to achieve
- format of each session
- who will be the leaders/facilitators
- outside homework (if any)
- refreshments (if any)
- visitors to the group
- social events
- confidentiality
- other items important to your group

Be as specific as possible as you think about what you want to do. Encourage the other members to share in the covenant process so that your group doesn't fall apart in three or four weeks because some of the group thought you were going to do something different. Your purpose with the covenant is to eliminate the hidden agendas and to help each person fully belong to the group.

Let me coach you a bit more. A once-a-week meeting is probably adequate. Meet for an hour to an hour-and-a-half. Probably ten to fifteen weeks is going to be long enough. Find the best time of day and the best day of the week for everybody.

A simple way to handle the content is to cover one chapter of the book each time, except the first and last weeks.

At your first meeting, focus on getting to know each other. Do some initial sharing, such as the generalities of job, family, Christian experience, reasons for wanting to join the group, and what each person hopes to get out of the group. Talk about the covenants and make sure that they are fully accepted. It might also be helpful to assign tasks to different people for the next meeting.

For the following weeks (two through fourteen), you could use a chapter a week for the content. The last week should be a wind-down session including evaluation and planning for the future.

Structures

Regarding format, I would suggest the following general structure:

1. 15 minutes—**share** what happened to you during the past week
2. 30 minutes—**discuss** a chapter of the book
3. 15 minutes—**practice** skills

4. 10 minutes—**pray** for each other

5. 5 minutes—**assign** tasks for next week

1. Sharing should be included each week. Group members can share something about what has happened in their lives during the past week related to the attitudes, qualities, and skills covered last week. Sharing will intensify the learning process and will help to sustain the week-by-week growth.

2. Discussion is the second segment of your time together. You should assume that each person has read the particular chapter or section under discussion. One person should be assigned each week to develop questions for the discussion. Good questions will not have yes, no, or simple answers. Good questions push people to wrestle with concepts, ideas, and problems which might not ordinarily be tackled. Good questions are tied to the development of all the friendship skills, qualities, and attitudes. Discussion time should flow logically into the skill-development time.

3. Skill development should be an important part of your time together. Someone should be assigned to oversee this segment so that the group can practice activities suggested in the book or activities that the skill-development leader for the week presents. Good skill exercises are activities that can be practiced in the group during the meeting, as well as by each individual during the following week.

4. Pray before the group disperses each week. Pray specifically for each other's work, family, other friends, church, community. It's okay to pray for the world, but be careful not to get too far off target. Your prayer time should be part of the process of helping each of you grow in relationships.

5. Assignments and homework should be expected because each person ought to be (a) reading between meetings, (b) practicing his or her skills, and (c) preparing for the next meeting.

Ideally, the group should share leadership by rotating responsibilities so that each person in the group has an opportunity to lead each of the five parts of the meeting.

Potential Problems

1. Inadequate covenants. If you invite your friends into a group by saying, "Hey, I'm getting a bunch of people together on Thursday nights for a while, would you guys like to come over?" Each person will come with his own agenda. One guy is coming to use your VCR and big screen TV. Another guy wants to shoot pool. One of the other guys hopes to spend some time working on your antique car. Unless the covenants are spelled out very completely, you can almost count on problems.

2. The third or fourth meeting. At this point, group members begin to feel that they know each other well and are committed to the group direction, or they want out because they misunderstood the original covenant. During that meeting, it might be helpful to bring up the covenant issues to make sure that everyone feels comfortable. Modify small areas to help everyone feel at ease.

3. Social events and visitors. Extra meetings outside your normal weekly structure are a good time for social events or visitors. If you try to turn the regularly scheduled weekly meeting into a pool party or trip to Disneyland, you may not accomplish either the social or the group purpose. Visitors to regular meetings will cause the group to regress. When a new person is present, everyone becomes more hesitant to share.

It is great to have social events. Social events can whet visitors' appetites for the friendships you are experiencing in your group.

Who knows, maybe when your group finishes this course, you could split up and start four new groups. Each of you from the original group could be facilitators of the new groups. What an impact that would have if each of you committed yourself to reproduce what you are experiencing! Gigantic changes would take place in families, businesses, communities, and churches, as well as in each person's life.

4. Winding down. Stopping is hard. It's better to plan when to stop and how to stop, rather than letting the group go on indefinitely and have members lose interest. Also, you all deserve a party to celebrate your growth as you end the group. So plan something special to commemorate your time together.

What of the Future?

Winding down is a problem, but it can best be solved by planning for the future. Would you like to stay together as a group and study another book, study a section of the Bible, or fix up a widow's house?

You may not want to leave each other. Why not continue to meet weekly, spending the early part of your time sharing together. Then split off into two to four groups. That way you can continue to enjoy each other, yet other people can share your joy and growth.

Planning the next step will help each person feel successful about concluding this group. Mapping out the future will help people to move beyond the loneliness and aimlessness that often occurs when a group breaks up.

I've experienced several close group relationships that have dramatically changed my life. I am especially indebted to three friends who were a part of my life at a very critical time.

A few years ago, I stood in the hallway of a hospital with Sally and our two oldest daughters, Barbara and Brenda. I listened to the doctor describe the unbelievable.

The white fluorescent light glared from the ceiling; the sterile white walls of the hall contrasted so sharply with the green surgical gown that the doctor wore.

The doctor tried to console me, but his words struck like a knife blow to my heart. Our youngest daughter, Becki, sixteen years old, just had her left leg amputated above midthigh. I had expected God to heal the malignant tumor and save her leg. But now she would be disabled for the rest of her life.

Would she be able to live a normal life? Would anyone want to marry her? These and other questions rushed through my mind in that horrible moment.

Even larger than my distress about Becki's future was the mushrooming gloom and despair I felt. I questioned God's power and the effectiveness of prayer. In the waiting room just behind us were fifty to seventy-five people who had come to be with us. They were representatives of the thousands of people who were praying for us.

Together we had been asking for healing. We had pleaded with God to intervene. Fasting and round-the-clock prayer meetings had taken place. Becki had been anointed with oil by the elders of the church. We had tried to follow everything Scripture teaches about healing.

Where was God? Why didn't he care? Why didn't he heal? Had I been deceived? Had I been deceiving other people? All of these years I had been telling people that God loved them and had a wonderful plan for their lives. I had proclaimed that all of the Bible was true.

I turned from the doctor. Sally followed me. We walked to the dead end of the hall. In frustration I started beating on the wall with my fists. Then I said to Sally, "Well, we're on our own now. God doesn't care about us. We'll have to take care of ourselves." I walked away from her and went down to the bottom of the hospital—to the morgue. I knew no one would be there. I belonged there. I felt like a dead man.

I sat on a bench outside the door of the morgue. Only death lay beyond those double doors. No other living being was there.

What had gone wrong? Why hadn't prayer worked? How was I supposed to go back to the church and tell those people that

God was alive and well? How could I ever again say that God was believable? After all, I'm not the one who thought up the idea of prayer. I'm not the one who dreamed up the concept of faith. It was God!

I felt betrayed. I felt like a mouse that had been pounced on by a cat, severely injured and unable to run away. But the cat— God—just kept slapping me back and forth between his paws.

As I sat there in despair and in theological confusion, I was aware of the presence of someone who had quietly walked up to stand beside me. For a long time he stood there without saying a word. Then he gently reached out his hand and put it on my shoulder.

He had a caring smile on his face as he said, "Conway, I've checked on Becki. She's okay. In fact, I'm not worried about her. I know her; she's a tough kid. She'll make it through this fine. But I'm worried about you. I'm also worried about all of the people who believe in you."

Dick was a pastor friend from another church in town. He was not offering Bible verses, pat answers, or a Pollyanna philosophy. He was just being a friend in the hour of my desperate need.

I felt as if I had fallen into a deep, deep hole. Dick quietly lowered himself into the hole to help me. Over the next few days two other men, Jim and Brock, also manned the rope that pulled me out of that pit of despair. They took turns with Dick, listening to my despair, anger, and anguish. They kept extending their friendship to me during those next grueling hours.

These were not men that I just bumped into. They were men with whom I had long-standing friendships. We had previously spent many hours talking, sharing, and praying together.

We had come to know and understand each other long before this heavy-duty situation came into my life.[4]

It's very difficult to become an instant friend when a person is in the middle of despair. But if someone has built a long-term relationship with another individual, it's possible for that person to step in at a crisis time and become the welcomed guest. My "friends" helped lift me from the pit of despair and restored me to a useful life.

Use the opportunities you have now in the good days to build relationships. If hard days come to your life or to your friends' lives, you will be able to easily step into each other's lives because you are already friends.

One final thought: Developing a friendship is a costly process—but without a friend who shares your innermost self, who loves you, and whom you can love—life is meaningless.

Notes

Chapter 1: Listen to Me

1. Norman Habel, *Interrobang* (Philadelphia: Fortress Press, 1969), 26–27.

Chapter 2: This Is Going to Be Fun!

1. Bruce Larson, *No Longer Strangers* (Waco, Tex.: Word, 1971), 93–94.
2. Martin Bolt and David G. Myers, *The Human Connection* (Downers Grove, Ill.: InterVarsity Press, 1984), 157.
3. Urie Bronfenbrenner, "Why Do the Russians Plant Trees Along the Road?" *Saturday Review* (January 1963), 96.
4. Galatians 5:22–23, *The Living Bible.*
5. Ephesians 4:7, 12–16, *The Living Bible.*
6. Robert C. Roberts, "Therapy for the Saints," *Christianity Today* (November 8, 1985), 25–26.
7. John 12:24, *New American Standard Bible.*

Chapter 3: Why We Like People/Why They Like Us

1. Ira Progoff, "The Psychology of Personal Growth," in Eric Butterworth, *You Make the Difference* (San Francisco: Harper & Row, 1984), 5.

2. David W. Johnson, *Reaching Out* (Englewood Cliffs, N.J.: Prentice-Hall, 1981), 5.

3. Mary Brown Parley and the editors of *Psychology Today,* "The Friendship Bond," *Psychology Today* (October 1979).

4. Martin Bolt and David G. Myers, *The Human Connection* (Downers Grove, Ill.: InterVarsity Press, 1984), 122.

5. Bolt and Myers, *The Human Connection,* 178.

6. Jim and Sally Conway, *Your Marriage Can Survive Mid-Life Crisis* (Nashville, Tenn.: Thomas Nelson, 1987), 7.

7. Bolt and Myers, *The Human Connection,* 125–28.

8. Bolt and Myers, *The Human Connection,* 178.

9. Philippians 2:6–7, *New American Standard Bible.*

10. 1 John 4:19, *King James Version.*

11. Matthew 9:11–12, *The Living Bible.*

12. John 15:15, *The Living Bible.*

13. Hebrews 4:16, *The Living Bible.*

14. Matthew 20:25–28, *New American Standard Bible.*

Chapter 4: What Do I Think of Myself?

1. Joyce Landorf, *Irregular People* (Waco, Tex.: Word, 1982).

2. Genesis 1:27, *King James Version.*

3. 2 Corinthians 5:17, *King James Version.*

4. 1 Corinthians 15:10, *New International Version.*

Chapter 5: The Maturing Person

1. Romans 12:3, *The Living Bible.*

2. 1 Corinthians 15:10, *King James Version.*

3. 1 Corinthians 15:10, *The Living Bible.*

4. John Powell, *Fully Human, Fully Alive* (Niles, Ill.: Argus Communications, 1976).

5. John 3:16–17, *The Living Bible.*

6. Alan B. Knox, *Adult Development and Learning* (San Francisco: Jossey-Bass, 1977), 354–55.

7. Duncan Buchanan, *The Counselling of Jesus* (Downers Grove, Ill.: InterVarsity Press, 1985), 81.

8. Buchanan, *The Counselling of Jesus,* 81–82.

9. Luke 19:8, *New American Standard Bible.*

10. Luke 19:9, *New American Standard Bible.*
11. For further information on these five traits see Erik H. Erikson, *Identity, Youth in Crisis* (New York: W. W. Norton, 1968); Stanley Coopersmith, *The Antecedents of Self-Esteem* (San Francisco: W. H. Freeman, 1967); and Keith and Gladys Hunt, *Not Alone* (Grand Rapids, Mich.: Zondervan, 1985).
12. 2 Corinthians 5:17, *The Living Bible.*
13. 2 Corinthians 12:9, *New American Standard Bible.*
14. See James 1:2–6; 2 Corinthians 11:23–12:10.

Chapter 6: Qualities That Build Friendships

1. Luke 23:43, *The Living Bible.*
2. Myron D. Rush, *Richer Relationships* (Wheaton, Ill.: Victor, 1983), 14.
3. Philippians 2:3–4, *New International Version.*
4. Bruce Larson, *No Longer Strangers* (Waco, Texas: Word Books, 1971), 101.
5. Philip Yancey, "Gandhi and Christianity," *Christianity Today* (April 8, 1983), 16.
6. Anthony Campolo, *The Power Delusion* (Wheaton, Ill.: Victor, 1983), 133.
7. Haim Ginott, *Between Parent and Child* (New York: Macmillan, 1965), 23–25.
8. Paul Tournier, *The Adventure of Living* (New York: Harper & Row, 1965), 66.
9. Julian B. Rotter, *Psychology Today* (October 1980), 35.
10. 1 John 4:16, *New International Version.*
11. John 13:34-35 *The Living Bible.*
12. Pitirim Sorokin, quoted in Eric Butterworth, *You Make the Difference* (San Francisco: Harper and Row, 1984).
13. John 15:13.
14. John Powell, *The Secret of Staying in Love* (Niles, Ill.: Argus Communications, 1974), 53.
15. John 15:13, *New International Version.*
16. Deuteronomy 6:7, *New American Standard Bible.*
17. Ann Kiemel, *I Love the Word Impossible* (Wheaton, Ill.: Tyndale House, 1976), 56.

Chapter 7: Skill #1—Attending: Focusing on Your Friend

1. Gerard Egan, *The Skilled Helper,* 3d ed. (Monterey, Calif.: Brooks/Cole, 1986), 75.
2. Albert Mehrabian, *Silent Messages* (Belmont, Calif.: Wadsworth, 1971), 4.
3. Patricia Noller, *Non-Verbal Communication and Marital Interaction* (Elmsford, N.Y.: Pergamon Press, 1984), 153.
4. A. Ivey, *Microcounseling: Innovations in Interviewing Training* (Springfield, Ill.: Charles C. Thomas, 1971), 93–94.
5. Egan, *The Skilled Helper,* 76.
6. Egan, *The Skilled Helper,* 76.
7. Egan, *The Skilled Helper,* 76.
8. Egan, *The Skilled Helper,* 76.
9. Gerard Egan, *Interpersonal Living* (Monterey, Calif.: Brooks/Cole, 1976), 98.

Chapter 8: Skill #2—Listening: One Part of Communication

1. Paul Tournier, *To Understand Each Other* (Atlanta: John Knox Press, 1967), 29–30.
2. Matthew 13:14, *The Living Bible.*
3. David Augsburger, *Caring Enough to Hear and Be Heard* (Ventura, Calif.: Regal, 1982), 29.
4. Luke 8:45, *New International Version.*
5. Duncan Buchanan, *The Counselling of Jesus* (Downers Grove, Ill.: InterVarsity Press, 1985), 32.
6. Buchanan, *The Counselling of Jesus,* 38–39.

Chapter 9: Skill #3—Talking: Another Part of Communication

1. Reuel Howe, *Herein Is Love* (Valley Forge, Penn.: Judson Press, 1961), 30.
2. David Augsburger, *Caring Enough to Hear and Be Heard* (Ventura, Calif.: Regal, 1982), 71–86.
3. Karen Rook, "UCI Psychologist Studies Why Many People Accentuate the Negative, Eliminate the Positive," *The Orange County Register* (January 6, 1986).

4. Hugh Prather, *Notes to Myself* (Moab, Utah: Real People Press, 1970).
5. Augsburger, *Caring Enough to Hear and Be Heard,* 29.
6. Sydney Gourard, *The Transparent Self* (New York: Van Nostrand Reinhold, 1971), 5.

Chapter 10: Skill #4—Empathy: Caring Enough to Send Your Very Best

1. *The Orange County Register,* (Friday, December 2, 1983), A16.
2. *The Orange County Register,* (Friday, December 2, 1983), D4.
3. Michael F. Isquick, "Training Older People in Empathy: Effects on Empathy, Attitudes, and Self-Exploration," *The International Journal of Aging and Human Development* vol. 13(1), 1981.
4. Martin Bolt and David G. Myers, *The Human Connection* (Downers Grove, Ill.: InterVarsity Press, 1984), 134.
5. Hebrews 4:14–16, *The Living Bible.*
6. Mark 1:41.
7. John 9:6.
8. Mark 5:41.
9. Mark 7:33.
10. Arthur W. Combs and Donald L. Avila, *Helping Relationships* (Newton, Mass.: Allyn and Bacon, 1985), 142.
11. Bolt and Myers, *The Human Connection,* 139.
12. Combs and Avila, *Helping Relationships,* 141.

Chapter 11: Skill #5—Genuineness: Being Real in a Phony World

1. Richard Schickel, "Peter Sellers," *Time* (March 3, 1980), 64.
2. John Powell, *Why Am I Afraid to Tell You Who I Am?* (Niles, Ill.: Argus Communications, 1969).
3. Carin Rubenstein and Phillip Shaver, *In Search of Intimacy: Surprising New Conclusions from a Nationwide Survey on Loneliness and What to Do About It* (New York: Delacorte Press, 1982), 24.
4. Genesis 2:18, *The Living Bible.*
5. Gerard Egan, *Interpersonal Living* (Monterey, Calif.: Brooks/Cole, 1976), 45.

Chapter 12: Skill #6—Affirmation: Passing on a Blessing

1. Carl Rogers, *The Therapeutic Relationship and Its Impact* (Madison, Wis.: University of Wisconsin Press, 1967), 102.
2. Gary Smalley and John Trent, *The Blessing* (Nashville, Tenn.: Thomas Nelson, 1986), 24.
3. Luke 6:32, 34–35, *New American Standard Bible.*
4. Ted W. Engstrom, *The Fine Art of Friendship* (Nashville, Tenn.: Thomas Nelson, 1985), 131–32.
5. See Exodus 20:5; 34:7; Numbers 14:18; Deuteronomy 5:9.
6. Matthew 11:29, *New International Version.*
7. Philippians 4:8, *New American Standard Bible.*
8. M. Mayerhoff, *On Caring* (New York: Perennial Library/Harper & Row, 1971), 41–42.
9. 1 John 4:19, *King James Version.*
10. Zephaniah 3:16b–18a, *The Living Bible.*
11. Helen Colton, *The Gift of Touch* (New York: Sea View Putnam, 1983), 102.
12. Colton, *The Gift of Touch,* 49.
13. Gayle Erwin, *The Jesus Style* (Palm Springs, Calif.: Ronald Haynes, 1983), 63.

Chapter 13: Putting It All Together

1. Margery Williams, *The Velveteen Rabbit* (Garden City, N.Y.: Doubleday, 1971), 16–17.
2. Williams, *The Velveteen Rabbit,* 24.
3. See Matthew 26; Mark 14; Luke 22; and John 13–17.
4. For a more complete account of my experience when Becki lost her leg, see the book *What God Gives When Life Takes* by Becki Conway Sanders, Jim and Sally Conway (Downers Grove, Ill.: InterVarsity Press, 1989).